Become a Better Software Architect - Actions and insights from practical experience

by Dr.-Ing. Kai Niklas

Get updates and news on
bettersoftwarearchitect.com

Dr.-Ing. Kai Niklas
Become a Better Software Architect - Actions and insights from practical experience

Publish date: May 2019
ISBN: 978-1-09-468474-1
Publisher: Independently Published

1st Edition

Feedback
I greatly appreciate any kind of feedback you have concerning this book. Please mail me at info@bettersoftwarearchitect.com

Dr.- Ing. Kai Niklas
Am Hegede
58313 Herdecke
Germany

Email: info@bettersoftwarearchitect.com
Website: https://bettersoftwarearchitect.com

Contents

Contents

Part I.

Foreword

1. About this book

Several years ago, I was asked: "How have you become a software architect?". We talked about necessary skills, experience and the amount of time and dedication it took to build up knowledge. Moreover, I went through the steps which I took. Which technologies I have worked with or tried out, and what I have learned during my professional and non-professional career.

This conversation has triggered myself and I started to structure the topics for my personal growth. "What makes a good software architect?", I wondered, and "How can I improve to become a better software architect?". I read articles and books, and of course talked with peers.

In this book, I want to share an overview of my insights with you. Which skills are most important, and how to improve them to become a (better) software architect.

This book addresses software engineers who want to learn and understand more about the work of an architect. Further, it gives insights for software architects who want to extend their existing knowledge.

1.1. What things will you learn?

The book is divided into two major sections:

▷ Understand the different *roles* and required *skills* of software architects

▷ *Insights* on how to improve the skills based on my personal experience

This book will not get into each detail but tries to give you a broad overview. Links to definitions, interesting books, videos or webpages are given to dig deeper into details there. It is not the goal of this book to describe each existing concept again. Only major concepts which are generating benefit within the context of this book will be described and discussed in more details. Many concepts are linked to the corresponding wikipedia article for quick look ups.

1.2. Focus on the human

From my experience, the human as such is highly important. Building up a "T" shape skill-set with broad and deep knowledge is important, but it is not enough to succeed in the domain of software engineering or architecture. Humans are building software, not machines. Humans need more than facts to build great software.

I personally feel, that the human is often forgotten. Not only in literature, but also in day to day life. Hence, I decided to write this book around a software architect: A human who is more than a walking book. I tried to balance this book between hard and soft skills in the area of software architecture.

1.3. Are the things proven to work?

The collection of insights, that are the foundation of this book, reflect my personal point of view, based on my experience of the last 15 years in IT. I try to be as unbiased as possible and refer to scientific sources whenever possible. Moreover, I give reading recommendations to further resources with similar or opposite thoughts, whenever applicable. This gives you the ability to decide by yourself if my saying is sound.

All actions and insights are written in small chunks, so that they are easy to consume and understand. Every chunk includes a description, the benefits, and at least one concrete example. With this you have a general applicable insight which can be adapted to your situation, as well as a demonstration on how to apply it. For many insights I added further readings to books or interesting web-pages.

Part II.

Introduction

2. The Software Architect

"Design and programming are human activities; forget that and all is lost."

(Bjarne Stroustrup)

To understand how a software architect can improve its skills, it is beneficial to recap what software architecture is and what a software architect does. For software architecture there are several good definitions. Further, it is important to also distinct between the traditional understanding of software architecture and *agile* software architecture. Based on definition, understanding of different specializations, flight levels and typical activities, the core skills every software architect should have is derived.

Contents

9

2.1. Definitions – Software Architect

Before diving into details, let's have a look at two definitions first to align on the term "software architecture" and what a software architect is:

> "**Software architecture** is the fundamental organization of a system, represented by its components, their relationships to each other and to the environment, and the principles that determine the design and evolution of the system." [72]

> "A **software architect** is a software expert who makes high-level design choices and dictates technical standards, including software coding standards, tools, and platforms. The leading expert is referred to as the chief architect." [89]

Agile Software Architecture

The classical definition for software architecture is still valid for agile software architecture. But there is one main difference: It's the mindset and the derived mechanics how to tackle architecture questions and design.

In the classical world, the whole design is determined at the very beginning. This is called Big Design Up Front (BDUF or BUFD) [63]. Within agile software development the concrete design decision is kept open as long as possible, until enough information is available and key learning have been made to decide on a concrete design. The assumption is, that at the beginning the functional and non-functional requirements are too vague to determine the concrete design.

Agile architecture evolves over time (growth mindset), whereas classic architecture is fixed at the very beginning (fixed mindset). If you want to learn more about the differences of those two mindsets, have a look at the following video:

 Growth Mindset vs. Fixed Mindset (YouTube) by John Spencer (http://bit.ly/2H0FBrg)

2.2. Architecture Flight Levels and Domains

Architecture is applied on several "flight levels" of abstractness. The level influences the importance of necessary skills. Different levels require different skills. Clustering or naming the levels can be done differently. I prefer the segmentation into these 3 levels:

▷ **Application Architecture:** The lowest level of architecture. Focus on one single application. Very detailed, low level design. Communication usually within one development team. Driven by concrete functional and non-functional requirements.

▷ **Solution Architecture:** The mid-level of architecture. Focus on one or more applications which fulfill a business need (business solution). Some high, but mainly low-level design. Communication between many development teams. Aligning functional and non-functional requirements with overarching business goals.

▷ **Enterprise Architecture:** The highest level of architecture. Focus on many solutions. High level, abstract design, which is detailed out by solution or application architects. Communication across the organization. Highly business goal driven.

Architects are often seen as the glue between different stakeholders. Three examples:

▷ **Horizontal**: Bridge communication between business and developers or different development teams.

▷ **Vertical**: Bridge communication between developers and managers or managers and senior management.

▷ **Technology**: Integrate different technologies or applications with each other.

Another dimension of architects is their specialization in a specific domain. Some common examples are:

▷ Software / Application

▷ Infrastructure / Network

▷ Database / Data

▷ Security

▷ Integration

▷ DevOps / Automation

▷ Business / Process

▷ Organization

Figure 2.1 puts all the dimensions together. Different architecture "specializations" can be applied on different levels. For example, a data architect on application level is concerned about data models within the application, whereas the data architect on enterprise level is driving the overall data-warehouse (DWH) initiative. Both are data architects, but with different goals and challenges.

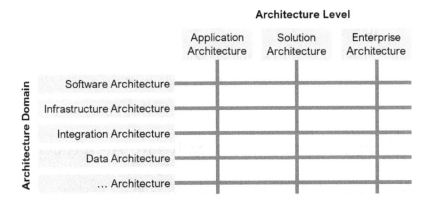

Figure 2.1.: Levels and domains of software architects

2.3. Typical Activities of Software Architects

To understand the necessary skills an architect needs, we need to understand typical activities. The following (non-final) list contains from my perspective the most important activities:

▷ Define and decide development technology and platform

▷ Define development standards, e.g., coding standards, tools, review processes, test approach, etc.

▷ Support identifying and understanding business requirements

▷ Design systems and take decisions based on requirements

▷ Document and communicate architectural definitions, design and decisions

▷ Check and review architecture and code, e.g., check if defined patterns and coding standards are implemented

▷ Collaborate with other architects and stakeholders

▷ Coach and consult developers

▷ Define, detail out and refine higher level design into lower level design

Note: Architecture is a continuous activity. Especially, when applied in agile software development. Thus, these activities need to be repeated.

2.4. Important Skills of Software Architects

To support the laid-out activities, specific skills are required. From my experience, read books and discussions, the skills every software architect should have can be boiled down to the following:

Design, Decide, Simplify, Code, Document, Communicate, Estimate, Balance, Coach, Consult, Market

Depending on the level of architecture, and the concrete role, some skills are more important than others. For example, an enterprise architect does not need to have deep coding skills. But an understanding of what developers are doing all day is helpful. Whereas application architects should be involved in coding. Hence, improving in this area is beneficial.

You can use this list as a compass to determine the areas in which you are strong and where you can potentially improve yourself. Let's go through one by one. For every skill I have laid out some actions or insights to follow up and to improve in that area.

Part III.

Skills of an Architect

3. Design – Theory

"If you think good architecture is expensive, try bad architecture."

(Brian Foote and Joseph Yoder)

What makes a good software design? This is one of the most often stated question I receive. I will make a distinction between design in theory and in practice. To my experience, having a mix of both is most valuable. Let's start with theory.

In this section you will learn more about the classic design patterns, patterns and anti-patterns in general and how they will help to create applications. Further, you will learn more about quality measures and metrics to increase understanding of why architects put an emphasize on design and non-functional requirements.

Contents

17

3.1. Know the basic design patterns

Design patterns are one of the most important tool architects need to have to develop maintainable code and systems. With patterns you can reuse design to solve common problems with proven solutions. Patterns are not libraries or functions which can be copy and pasted. They are rather solution blueprints and need to be implemented and adapted to the realities in the code.

Benefits

Design patterns are a toolkit of *tried and tested solutions* to common problems in software design. Knowing patterns is useful as it teaches how to solve various problems, e.g., using principles of object-oriented design.

Design patterns define a *common language*, which is helpful to communicate more efficiently. Further, you can build on top of existing knowledge and adapt to your problems.

Example

Let's assume you want to lay out the code structure for a user interface, have little experience and using no frameworks. You start programming, and after every iteration and every new feature, it gets harder and harder to maintain the code. At this point you may ask yourself: "I am not the first person on earth who did something like that. Isn't there a common solution to structure code for front-ends?". And the answer is yes. There are many patterns to structure your front-end code, e.g., Model-View-Controller (MVC) [109]. With MVC you get a very clear structure of the code. And the best is, that everyone who already knows MVC understands your code as well.

You may say, that MVC is old and outdated. But the base concept of MVC is still valid, and it is still around in many applications and frameworks. For example, the framework "Spring MVC" is using it as its base architecture. Based on MVC, new patterns emerged which are used in recent frameworks, e.g. Model View ViewModel (MVVM)[110] is used in Angular, Ember.js, Vue.js, ReactJS, etc.

Further Reading

▷ **Design Patterns: Elements of Reusable Object-Oriented Software** [30] written by the "Gang of Four" (GoF) is one of the most important books about design patterns, and a must read to everyone who is in software development. Although, the patterns were published more than 20 years ago, they are still the basis of modern software architecture.

 Find an overview of popular patterns on wikipedia (http://bit.ly/2PPuW5B)

3.2. Dig deeper into patterns and anti-pattern

If you already know the basic GoF patterns, then extend your knowledge with more software design patterns. Or dig deeper into your area of interest.

Additionally, learn about anti-patterns, which are the opposite of patterns. Whenever they occur in your design, the risk is high, that the solution will be ineffective or leads to massive problems.

Important: Patterns and anti-patterns are not only applicable to design, e.g., object-oriented programming. You can find them everywhere, e.g., enterprise organization, project management, software design, software development, software maintenance, programming, configuration management and many more.

Benefits

Having the knowledge of patterns, especially in your domain, helps you to get your work done more efficiently. The experience you made by yourself is probably the most important. But your time is limited, and you cannot try out everything by yourself. You need to rely on others. Patterns are a great source of knowledge. Especially, those written by trustworthy people, including their rationale.

With anti-patterns you can more easily stop implementations or behaviors which are leading into the wrong direction. Your gut feeling will most likely tell you, that something is wrong with the design, but you cannot find the right arguments. With anti-patterns this is easier, as they often come with concrete examples.

Important: Patterns and anti-patterns are important, but it is easy to over-engineer and apply too many patterns. This will lead to ineffective systems. I observed this once in an university project where they tried to solve every problem with a pattern. I would call that an anti-pattern, too. Keep the right balance.

Example – Pattern Deep Dive

If your job or interest is to integrate applications with each other, then you could do a research for common patterns and anti-patterns. As said above, you are not the first person on earth and you should build on top of existing knowledge to avoid mistakes others did already. For application integration the book "Enterprise Integration Patterns" [39] written by Gregor Hohpe is a great source for patterns.

This book is applicable in various areas, whenever two applications need to exchange data. Whether it is an old-school file exchange from some legacy systems or a modern microservice architecture.

Example – Anti-Patterns

You can find many resources of design anti-patterns. Especially, the "new" way of building applications in a microservice architecture style has many pitfalls. To succeed with microservices, patterns and anti-patterns are very helpful to better understand the mechanics and what to avoid in your design. Often you do not see the impact of your decisions in the early stage of development, but late, when it gets costly to change.

One good resource to get you started is for example the book Microservices antipatterns and pitfalls [73] by Mark Richards. Mark lays out 10 common anti-patterns and pitfalls and provides solutions to avoid them.

There are many more resources for anti-patterns. Not only in the design area. But also, for software development itself. For example Stefan Wolpers described roughly 160 Scrum Anti-Patterns in his guide [127].

Further Reading

▷ **Enterprise Integration Patterns** [39] by Gregor Hohpe

▷ Microservices antipatterns and pitfalls [73] by Mark Richards

▷ Scrum Anti-Patterns Guide [127] by Stefan Wolpers

3.3. Know quality measures and metrics

Defining and applying architecture is not an end in itself. There are good reasons why patterns, guidelines and coding standards are defined, applied and controlled. It is to build high quality software products.

Software quality has various definitions. For the context of this book I would like to highlight the following two closely related notions (compare [120]):

> ▷ **Software functionality:** Indicates how good the software fulfills functional requirements or business needs. This is tightly related with the term *fit to purpose*, which stands for how ideal the software is for the given use and context.

> ▷ **Software structure:** Indicates how good the software meets non-functional requirements, which directly influence the delivery of the functional requirements, e.g., maintainability or extensibility.

There are many quality measures for different purposes. Probably the most known and common measures are the following, according to ISO 9126 [103], but there are many more:

> ▷ **Functionality:** Suitability, Accuracy, Interoperability, Security

> ▷ **Reliability:** Maturity, Fault tolerance, Recoverability

> ▷ **Usability:** Understandability, Learnability, Operability, Attractiveness

> ▷ **Efficiency:** Time behavior, Resource utilization

> ▷ **Maintainability:** Analyzability, Changeability, Stability, Testability

> ▷ **Portability:** Adaptability, Installability, Co-existence, Replaceability

To meet non-functional as well as functional requirements, the following actions can be taken:

1. **Patterns & Guidelines**: The usage of proven patterns and avoidance of anti-patterns can help to increase non-functional requirements. For every quality aspect, specific guidelines can be defined, e.g., write and document code in a specific way so that it stays maintainable.

2. **Static code analysis (SCA):** At design time it is possible to check the code automatically against common coding standards or calculate metrics. The most prominent example where we can see this live in action is Eclipse. During coding the IDE is constantly checking not only the syntax, but applies additional checks, which for example detect missing exception handling or potential null-pointer issues. One popular tool for managing and checking code regularly is SonarQube [80].

3. **Dynamic (runtime) analysis:** Unfortunately, software cannot be judged solely by analyzing the code. Thus, it is necessary to run and "play" with the software (system). Performance analysis, security testing, or memory leak detection are three examples which run the software and simultaneously capture data to identify the potential cause within the code.

4. **Chaos Engineering:** Playing and experimenting with software systems in production gained some popularity recently, to build confidence of the system's capability to handle unexpected conditions. Chaos Monkey [60] by Netflix is one popular tool which can for example shut down servers automatically and test the fault tolerance of the system.

Benefits

Often developers or architects do not understand or even know the reasons why they are applying and following specific architecture styles, patterns or guideline. This leads to frustration and ignorance. If you are only told to do something, you are unlikely or even unwilling to follow. This does not help to craft good software. But if you can give reasons, it helps to establish the right mindset. Of course, the initial effort is higher, but in the long run, you will gain the benefits, as everyone has understood and applies it. Physiologic experiments demonstrate, that providing reasons to kids why they should not take a specific toy is twice as effective in the long run as simply forcing them to not take the toy[1].

With static code analysis tools, e.g., SonarQube, you can measure code and detect potential problems. You can do this continuously and integrate it into your automation tools, e.g., Jenkins. You could even define a threshold and stop deployments or releases if the quality is too low based on the defined metrics.

When applying static or dynamic code analysis tools, it is important to set the right mindset with developers and managers. It is not about controlling people or teams. It is not about judging that one team is better than another. It is not about monetary penalties for external vendors. The reason is, to support and help developers to create better software.

Note: If the culture and mindset in your company cannot handle transparency and handling errors well, I would discourage from introducing such tools. A missing mindset will start quality discussions and reduce the overall productivity and moral. Thus, first establish the mindset.

Example – Testability

The more often you want to release your software, the more needs to be automated, so that you can assure the speed of delivery and

---

[1] Unfortunately, I do not find the source for that experiment. It was stated by Vera F. Birkenbihl, a German management trainer and author in one of her great talks.

quality. For example, amazon released already in 2011 their software every 11.6 seconds[2].

In particular, the automation includes test automation. You are not only testing code fully automatically, but also the environments. Hence, software, and even environments, need to be build in a way that they are testable. One popular solution is to use docker, so that the environment looks the same everywhere.

To achieve a high testability of software, guidelines and patterns are also important. For example, the usage of interfaces in combination with dependency injection allows to exchange classes during test runs with mocks. Mocks could for example return dummy values, instead of establishing a connection to a database, or simulate network outages by returning an error after a longer period.

One option to measure testability at design time is to measure the "Cyclomatic Complexity", which calculates the complexity of software [56]. The metric calculates how many linear independent paths the code can take. The more paths the code can take, the more test cases are necessary to have a proper test coverage. It is possible to reduce the complexity by breaking down complex code into smaller pieces and hence, simplify testing.

Further Reading

▷ **Introduction to Software Quality** [65] by Gerard O'Regan

▷ **Metrics and Models in Software Quality Engineering** [43] by Stephen Kan

▷ **Chaos Engineering** [74] by Rosenthal et al.

---

[2]https://news.ycombinator.com/item?id=2971521

4. Design – Practice

> *"Perfection (in design) is achieved not when there is nothing more to add, but rather when there is nothing more to take away"*

(Antoine de Saint-Exupery)

Theory is important as well as practice. It is hard to keep up with the speed new technology emerges. And while I'm writing this sentence, the chance is high that a new JavaScript framework was released. This sounds like a joke, but it feels very real [2]. But at least, you should try to keep up-to-date with new technologies, especially technology stacks. And not only on a theoretical level. Try them out and get a feeling what they are all about: Their benefits as well as their downsides, e.g., their maturity.

In this section I give you a glimpse on different technology stacks, an example on learning patterns by analyzing them practically and the importance of curiosity to learn new things and taking responsibility during implementation.

Contents

4.1. Try out and understand different technology stacks

This may be one of the most important activity if you want to become a better software architect. Try out (new) technology stacks and learn their ups and downs. Different or new technology comes with different design aspects and patterns. You most likely do not learn much from flipping through abstract slides, but by trying it out by yourself and feel the pain or the relieve. An architect should not only have broad, but also in some areas deep knowledge. The typical "T" shape. It is not important to master all technology stacks, but to have a solid understanding of the most important in your area.

Also try out technology which is not in your area, e.g., if you are deep into SAP R/3 you should also try JavaScript and vice versa. Someone who has only seen ABAP code and SAP software will be surprised about the power of code versioning with GIT. Whereas someone who has never seen SAP will be delighted by the stability of the whole framework. Still, both parties will be surprised about the latest advances in SAP S/4 HANA.

Benefit

Knowing different technologies or technology stacks is beneficial when it comes to problem solving. Technology is advancing fast and different kind of technologies are trying to solve different kind of problems. They introduce new patterns or even paradigms. In the best case, they are not only introducing it, but also practically prove to be valid and beneficial. With this knowledge at hand, it will be easier to find solutions for your specific problems or to introduce a standard approach to your problem.

One common phenomenon which I sometimes observe among architects and usually among developers is, that they tend to stick to solutions which they know, without having a serious look at alternative approaches or technologies. And of course, it is not necessary to jump on every new train. But a "one-size-fits-all" approach is also not the solution. If you ask a colleague with a strong background in databases, the solution will most likely be DB centric. If this person has a strong Oracle background, then it will most likely be an Oracle DB.

Thus, remember the following: "If all you have is a hammer, everything looks like a nail." [55] This cite goes back to Abraham Maslow, a psychologist, in 1966. And it is so true today. If your tool-set is limited, you will try to solve everything with what you have, although there may be better alternatives.

Note: It is important to find the right balance between reusing existing tools and introducing new tools. Obviously, it is not the best option to introduce for every problem a new tool. On the other hand, it is not smart to solve everything with the same "hammer". You need to find the right balance.

Examples – LAMP, MEAN, ELK

Let's have a look at three quite popular software stacks, which are good examples to know and study further:

> **LAMP** (Linux, Apache, MySQL, PHP). This stack is used for creating websites and web-applications with a relational DB and PHP. PHP is still widely used although it is not "hip" anymore. For example WordPress is programmed in PHP, which powers 32% of the web, based on statistics provided by Automattic, the company behind WordPress [128]. Typical adaptions to this stack are:

  – Operation System: Windows instead of Linux (WAMP)

  – Web-Server: NGINX instead of Apache

     – Relational DB: MariaDB or PostgreSQL instead of MySQL

▷ **MEAN** (MongoDB, Express, Angular, node.js). Like the LAMP stack it is all about web-sites and web-applications, but using NoSQL DBs, e.g., document, key-value or graph based, and JavaScript for server-side and client-site code. Popular adaptions to this stack are:

     – NoSQL DB: PostgresSQL[1], Neo4j as graph DB or Redis for key-value stores instead or as addition to a MongoDB.

     – Front-End: React or Vue.js instead of Angular

▷ **ELK** (elasticsearch, logstash, kibana). This stack is often used for log analytics in environments with many applications. "Elasticsearch is a search and analytics engine. Logstash is a server-side data processing pipeline that ingests data from multiple sources simultaneously, transforms it, and then sends it to a 'stash' like Elasticsearch. Kibana lets users visualize data with charts and graphs in Elasticsearch." [24]

Example – SAP S/4Hana

That I include S/4Hana, as a technology stack, is something which may be a bit surprising at first. But it is a solid example of how even perceived dinosaurs can innovate, and it is worth to try out, not only for the enterprise. SAP Hana is more than a new type of database. With its in-memory capabilities and new way of managing data (e.g., columns instead of rows) it dramatically increases performance of queries and enables to reduce layers which are required in classic

---

[1]Although PostgreSQL is well known in the relational DB area, it can be used as replacement for MongoDB as document oriented DB with some trade-offs. "postgres and mongodb are not fully compatible, but a JSONB column in postgres is conceptually a document – not just text, but fully parsed and indexable data, that can be manipulated with special operators." (Source: https://github.com/zalando/tech-radar/issues/13)

enterprise data-warehouse applications (staging area, persistence of aggregations, universe, etc.). This simplifies application design and reduces development as well as maintenance effort.

As said, it is more than a DB. It is a platform, which comes with application servers to run node.js or java applications, serve REST or OData services for front-ends, e.g., UI5, Angular or React, and connectors to integrate any source system, e.g., files, external DBs or streams of data. It provides a bunch of services which can be integrated additionally: From simple logging utilities to machine learning. And of course, you can communicate from every part within the platform with the database itself.

You can try it out by yourself and take a course at openSAP[2] for free. Be curious and try out new things. Also try out stuff which you did not liked some years ago.

4.2. Analyze and understand applied patterns

Reading about patterns is interesting (and at the same time boring). Trying patterns in a sandbox environment is more fun and more sustainable. Unfortunately, we cannot try out each pattern. We do not have so much time. And reading only is also not the solution. One "shortcut" which I found for myself, is to analyze open source frameworks and their used patterns.

Benefit

Frameworks usually come with some documentation which explain how to use their code. Sometimes they also explain design principles and applied patterns. These frameworks are interesting to examine.

---

[2]https://open.sap.com

To try out the patterns, all you must do is read the documentation and apply them accordingly to the framework. Less boilerplate code and no cumbersome implementation of the pattern itself is needed. This increases time to analyze the properties of the pattern.

The second benefit is, to see the pattern in a real environment. In a sandbox implementation it's interesting to study the basic mechanics. But analyzing and experiencing it within a framework is different. It provides more insights as the interplay with business logic and/ or other patterns are included.

Example – Angular and RxJS

At university I learned the first basic patterns. Among them the Observer pattern. I also programmed and analyzed the pattern in Java. But I was not aware of the full potential of the pattern, if used more extensively. In Angular[3] I experienced Observables[4] the first time in combination with RxJS[5], a library for reactive programming[6]. Reactive programming is a programming paradigm "concerned with data streams and the propagation of change" [118]. RxJS is a JavaScript library which uses Observables to enable this asynchronous or callback-based programming style.

It is not only interesting to use Observables, but also to understand how it was implemented. And there are tons of examples on how to use them. I think, that this pattern and reactive style of programming will be with us for the next years. Therefore, I highly recommend studying it further.

---

[3]https://angular.io/
[4]https://angular.io/guide/observables
[5]https://angular.io/guide/rx-library
[6]https://en.wikipedia.org/wiki/Reactive_programming

4.3. Be curious and attend User Groups

People with similar interests are organizing themselves within User Groups all around the globe and meet themselves on a regular basis. People discuss and present their ideas, challenges, solutions and approaches to various topics often related to a specific topic of their group.

Benefit

While attending User Groups you are not only able to extend your professional network, but also to strengthen your skills, knowledge and thinking outside the box. Some topics may only strive your interests, some may be spot on your current challenges. Topics which you would never start exploring by yourself are discussed and may inspire you. Topics which are of your interest may strengthen your expertise. You can only win.

Example – Java User Groups

Java User Groups are a great point to start. They are usually open to all kind of topics which have at least something to do with Java or architecture topics. To my knowledge these Groups are organized all around the globe and you most likely will find one in the next bigger city. And if not, you could to start one, and start exchanging ideas with your peers.

4.4. Take responsibility during implementation

This topic is especially for application and solution architects important. If you are too far away from the actual work, meaning development, you may become an Ivory Tower Architect [77]. Ivory tower architects are those who know a lot in theory but are detached from reality or have little or no practical experience. And as they are not responsible for the delivery, they are also less concerned about the impact their decision will have on the development. Developers often hesitate to take advises or decisions serious of ivory tower architects. The main reason is that they are too far away and do not know the challenges developers have to fulfill the functional and non-functional requirements.

Benefit

If you do not want to become an ivory tower architect, then you better be part of the development team(s). As technology is changing rapidly, it is easy to become an ivory tower architect, unless you invest some time into practical (and theoretical) training. This will ground and improve your decisions, developers will take you seriously and you are able to continuously learn to eventually become an evangelist (if you are interested and dedicated enough).

Hence, my advice is to take responsibility and support design, be available during implementation or write code and fix your own failures. This is a solid way to not get too far away from development.

Example

No example. Just do it.

5. Decide

"Language design and implementation is engineering. We make decisions using evaluations of costs and benefits or, if we must, using predictions of those based on past experience."

(Daniel Kahneman)

An architect needs to be able to take decisions and guide projects, product development, or the entire organization into the right direction. To take the right, or at least a good decision, some techniques and tools are available to support that exercise. It is not enough to solely rely on your knowledge and experience.

In this section I give you my view on what is important when it comes to architecture decisions, how you can prioritize work, conduct evaluations of architecture options and understand when to decentralize the decision-making process.

Contents

5.1. Know what is important

Do not waste time with "unimportant" decisions or activities. Learn what is important. Focus on decisions which may have big impacts and can for example dramatically increase (or decrease) development speed or quality. For myself, I found the following two principles to be most important to estimate the importance of a decision:

▷ **Conceptional Integrity:** If you have defined a guiding principle, you should stick to it, even if it is sometimes better to do it differently. This leads to a more straightforward, overall concept, eases comprehensibility and maintenance.

▷ **Economic View:** Every decision should be made economically, which means to incorporate the monetary impact of decisions and the expected outcome.

Benefit

Knowing what is important saves yourself and your company time, money and headaches. You probably have experienced lengthy and awkward discussions, e.g., about naming conventions, if it is better to use upper- or lowercase for specific kind of variables. Based on your organization's culture, this can go back and forth for weeks, and at the end, neither decision has a significant impact on the development speed nor quality. But it has wasted a lot of time and energy. It is a minor decision. You can be better by stopping such kind of discussions: "Do whatever you prefer but do it in the same way everywhere." If there is an industry standard or default, then stick to that, e.g., Java coding style, SAP naming conventions, etc. If there is a constraint in technology, then obey to the constraint, e.g., lengths of field names in databases.

The principle of conceptual integrity is further motivated by the observation, that local optimization usually does *not* lead to global optimization [48]. Think about performance optimization. It is often possible to tweak a method to be faster by violating some guiding principles, but the whole process chain is still slow. And another developer will struggle to understand your code. It would be more beneficial to analyze the process chain end-to-end and take the decision on how to optimize globally.

Both principles are especially important in agile development environments. Quick decisions for minor aspects are better than months of discussions without any decision. You can adapt and refactor later, after you have made some learning and experience. On the other hand, major, fundamental decisions, should be taken more wisely. Not only from a technical, but also from an economic perspective. If you can earn a lot of money by being the first in the market, you should make this a priority over endless naming convention discussions.

Example – Vendor Strategy

This example is more for the enterprise architects among us. If you have defined the strategy to go with a specific vendor, then you should stick to it, and do not scatter your landscape, unless you have actively decided to eliminate the principle. Sticking to your past decisions if they are valid, is usually a good thing. No major decisions need to be taken, everyone knows the direction, and the goals which are connected to the principle are more likely to become true. No one needs to waste time.

5.2. Learn to Prioritize

Some decisions are highly critical. If they are not taken early enough, workarounds pile up, which are unlikely to be removed later and are a

nightmare for maintenance. Or worse, developers simply stop working until a decision is taken. In such situations it is even better to
go with a "bad" decision instead of having no decision. But before it
comes to this situation, consider prioritizing upcoming decisions to
prevent this crisis.

There are different ways to achieve good prioritization. I suggest to
use the Weighted Shortest Job First (WSJF) [75] model for prioritizing jobs, based on the economics of product development flow [71].
This prioritization method gained popularity within the scaled agile software development framework (SAFe). But it is also applicable
outside of SAFe.

The formulas to calculate WSJF are the following:

$$\text{WSJF} = \frac{\text{Cost of Delay (CoD)}}{\text{Job size}}$$

$$\text{CoD} = \frac{\text{Business}}{\text{Value}} + \frac{\text{Time}}{\text{Criticality}} + \frac{\text{Risk Reduction or}}{\text{Opportunity Enablement}}$$

All variables need to be *relatively* estimated with values ranging, e.g.,
from 1 to 100. The numbers are not person days or amount of money,
but relatively "factors" between the jobs. For example, a job with size
of 2 takes twice as long as a job with size 1. The process to estimate
can be done like planning poker in agile software development, but
with more variables.

The job with the highest WSJF value is the one which should be tackled first. It has a high CoD and a small job size; thus, it can be finished
fast. In systems with fixed resources, the job size is a good proxy for
the duration.

The cost of delay is important to highlight. The sum of business
value, time criticality and risk reduction respectively opportunity en-
ablement results in CoD. The CoD reflects the value of the job, and

the longer you wait to implement it, the more "costs" it causes, e.g., by a missed opportunity to safe money or scale the application.

For prioritizing architecture topics and open decisions (the jobs), estimating time criticality and risk reduction is most important. Business value is hard to estimate for technical topics, why some people omit it. The job size is the estimate of how long the decision-making process takes.

Benefit

Ranking architecture topics and open decisions using WSJF enables you to produce the maximum economic benefit. Decisions with a high CoD and small job size will naturally be prioritized higher, whereas items with low CoD and high job size will be last.

One interesting thing is, that low priority decisions sometimes vanish over time, as they are getting obsolete. And the good thing is, that this is totally fine. There is usually more work to do than people picking it up.

Note: This method appears to be heavy, but it is not. You go through your list of topics and estimate. They do not need to be highly accurate. The first prioritization list may appear counter intuitive, but after reading the example below, you will realize, that this method may perform better than your gut feeling. You need to give it a try.

Bonus: One major aspect which is often forgotten when talking about WSJF is the gained alignment while executing the prioritization. You may think: "Why do I need to iterate over the items so many times?". This is exactly the alignment. You talk about the same items from different angles and gain, respectively share, insights. With this, knowledge is distributed and the work on the items will be eased within a larger group.

Example – WSJF

The following example demonstrates how the prioritization of jobs works and which economic benefit it has. Table 5.1 includes three jobs A, B and C with different job size and CoD. WSJF has the assumption / simplification of interpreting the size a proxy variable for the duration: Bigger jobs take longer than smaller jobs.

Job	Size	CoD	WSJF
A	1	10	10
B	5	5	1
C	10	1	0.1

Table 5.1.: Example of WSJF calculation

If you now start to work on the highest WSJF first, you can minimize the cost of delay. That means, the risk of a late decisions can be reduced and most critical decisions are taken first. Whereas working on the lowest WSJF first causes a high cost of delay. Still, in both cases you need the same time to complete the work. Figure 5.1 is illustrating this effect (compare [71]).

On the left side of Figure 5.1 you start working on the jobs with the *highest* WSJF. Hence, job A is completed first within 1 unit of time causing no CoD. Then job B can be started. As it starts 1 unit after A with a CoD of 5, it causes costs of $1 \cdot 5 = 5$. C needs to wait for A and B for $1 + 5 = 6$ units of time with a CoD of 1. Therefore, C causes the cost of 6. Overall, this prioritization causes a delay cost of 11.

On the right side of Figure 5.1 you start working on the jobs with the *lowest* WSJF. While working on C, A and B have to wait. A waits 10 units of time and B $10 + 5 = 15$ units of time. Multiplied by their CoD, this results in $10 \cdot 5 = 10$ cost of delay for B and $15 \cdot 10 = 150$ costs for A. Overall 200.

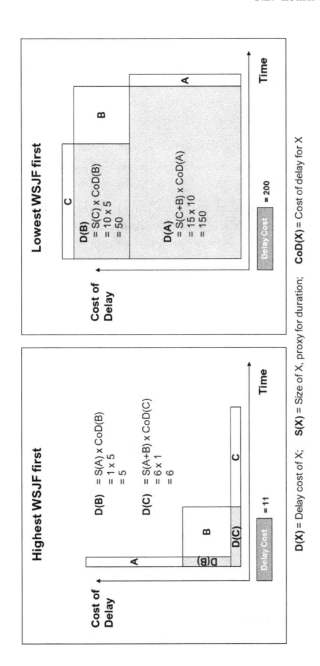

Figure 5.1.: Comparison of highest vs. lowest WSJF

41

The delay cost is just an artificial calculated number. But this number has a meaning. It represents missed business value or opportunities which could not be achieved. The longer you wait, the higher the risks are that the initiative comes too late and can't unfold it's full potential.

Important: The values for CoD and size are estimated *relatively*. That means, you compare the items with each other, instead of assigning absolute values.

Variations: If you prefer a more "agile" way of estimating the jobs, you could use the modified Fibonacci numbers, and play planning poker. Alternatively, put all items on a post-it and put the first on a wall. Take the next, and ask the group: higher or lower. Do this, until you have put all items on the wall. Then assign numbers based on the ordering. Repeat it for all required WSJF variables.

Further Reading

▷ **The principles of product development flow: second generation lean product development** [71] by Donald Reinertsen

5.3. Evaluate multiple options

Always lay out more than one option if it comes to decisions. In many cases I was involved in, there was more than one possible (good) option. Going with only one option is bad in two aspects:

▷ It seems that you did not do your job properly

▷ It impedes making proper decisions

Additionally, you should add measures to the options to enable a proper comparison based on facts instead of gut feelings, e.g. license costs or maturity. This usually leads to better and more sustainable decisions. Further, it eases to sell the decision to different stakeholders. Besides, if you do not have evaluated options properly you may miss arguments when it comes to discussions.

Benefit

Evaluation of options based on proper measures is one of the key tools every architect should master. It gives you a structured approach to come to decisions. As said above, gut feelings will not convince people. Companies are looking for architects who can make the decision-making process transparent to understand and steer more efficient.

The bigger the impact of the decision which needs to be taken, the better it needs to be prepared. There is nothing more embarrassing than going to your CIO and telling about your gut feeling.

Evaluating is not limited to draw options on paper, but also to try out and implement solution in form of spikes or proof of concepts. This enables you to learn and understand the impacts even better. At best this is done together with the development team(s).

Example – Option paper outline

Good option paper includes at least the following items:

  ▷ **Initial situation**: What is the initial situation?

  ▷ **Business and IT drivers**: What are the functional and non-functional requirements of the solution?

  ▷ **Consequences of no action**: What are the consequences if no decision is taken?

  ▷ **Solution space**: What was done to come to the proposed options and solutions? What where alternatives which were discarded?

▷ **Options**: List of options with their details: What is the option about? Including textual description, diagrams, etc. Which impacts, and consequences will the decision have?

▷ **Assessment**: Conduct a SWOT (Strengths, Weaknesses, Opportunities, Threats) analysis for all options [121]. Define, evaluate and compare all options based on objective criteria, e.g., realizing of functional and non-functional requirements, economic view (costs, effort), risks, future orientation, conformity to business and IT strategy, etc.

▷ **Recommendation**: Lay out the recommendation and justification based on the conducted evaluation.

Of course, it is not necessary to include all the mentioned items above in every option paper and to dig very deep into the details. You need to grow a feeling for the importance of the decision and the investment into the corresponding evaluation.

5.4. Know your competence

Within organizations you can often observe hierarchies. And yes, even if today's organizations claim to have flat hierarchies and decentralized decision-making processes, these hierarchies are still there. It is even more complex, as within projects or teams, specific group dynamics arise. That means, specific roles, norms, values, communication patterns and status differences are formed [101].

Therefore, do not decide things which are not in your competence. This is critical as it may ruin your position as architect significantly if not considered. To avoid this, clarify which responsibilities you have and what is part of your role. If there is more than one architect, then you should also clarify who is doing what and respect the level of architecture and domain in which you are currently deployed. As a lower level architect, you better come up with suggestions instead of decisions for higher level architecture and vice versa. Further, I recommend checking critical decisions always with another architect.

This sounds intimidating at first. It does not mean that you should shy away and be super cautious. But you need to find the right working mode and place within the organization, project or team first, before pushing too hard.

Benefit

As architect you want to push topics forward and generate value for the company, project, product, team, etc. Pushing too hard or in the wrong way, will not give you any benefits. The opposite is the case. It can be even be a career limiting move by ignoring social group dynamics.

Clarifying responsibilities with your peers establishes a more productive work environment. This way, it is easier to push topics forward which are in your territory. And topics which are outside of your responsibility are not actively on your mind anymore which saves energy. Further, you can clearly position yourself within the organization and become the go-to person for specific topics.

Scientific studies demonstrate that knowing your place within a social group has positive effects on your work and health [130]. Knowing your place within an organization is motivational and activates similar regions in your brain as monetary rewards [130]. Thus, this should be the first thing to do in a new or changed environment.

Example – Decision making process

Before you take any decision by yourself, just because you are "the architect", clarify how decisions are taken. Is there a group, who needs to be informed first? What about the developers who are directly affected? Are you a service provider and need a sign-off by your client? Only if the important parameters are clarified, and your position and responsibilities are clear, you may get into a productive working mode. Before that, my advice is to stay conservatively, and work out proposals and options and discuss them with your colleagues around you instead of taking decisions alone.

5.5. Decentralized decisions

It is hard to decide and describe everything (upfront). Especially, if you have decided to apply agile software development, big up-front design (BUFD [63]) is hardly meaningful. Especially, if multiple agile teams are involved, a centralized architecture team who decides on everything is not working. It creates a bottleneck and silo team, in which concepts are produced, often too far away from the current needs. It's also against one of the core ideas of agile software development, having self-organized, cross-functional and empowered teams which can run on their own.

Since a couple of years, the notion of a VUCA world is gaining popularity [25]. VUCA [124] stands for Volatility, Uncertainty, Complexity and Ambiguity. It is actually a term which originated in the 90's. But it's describing well the environment in which we are currently living and working in. To cope with these attributes new approaches are emerging. In such an environment it is hard to have a team who takes all decisions centrally. Thus, more and more decisions need to be decentralized.

Depending on your goals, you should actively decide when to apply decentralized and centralized decision making. The following factors gives you an indication (according to [64, 84]):

▷ **Responsiveness through immediacy**: Taking the right action quickly in order to respond to a challenge or opportunity. Take the decision where the work is done, e.g., within the team. The information is where the work is done. This is when to apply decentralized decision-making.

▷ **Reliability through compliance**: Some decisions need to be taken centrally, as they are prescribed by regulations or even laws, e.g., security related questions.

▷ **Efficiency through syndication**: A centralized unit is working more economically if they aggregate work which otherwise would be done separately. Three examples where it makes sense to centralize decision making:

  – **Economies of scale**: Providing and operating infrastructure is better done within a centralized team than by individual groups. It leads to standardization, specialization and increased productivity.

  – **Minimum efficient scale**: Scarce expertise which is required only sometimes by a team. Better group these people in a central group instead of replicating them in each group.

  – **Avoiding duplication**: Common needs which are for all solutions nearly identical, e.g., infrastructure.

▷ **Long-term goals through detachment**: Some decisions may harm the overall success and direction of a company. Projects or product teams often have only a short-term sight and objective, which they want to achieve and are not interested in the mid- or long-term goals. They may not even know them. Thus, some strategic decisions need to be taken within a centralized, company-wide group. Local (decentralized) optimization does not lead to to global optimization [48]. More on this in Section 11.2.

Rule of thumb: If the decision is time critical, and decisions on the topic are required frequently, and no "economy of scale" is in-place, then this is a candidate for decentralized decision-making.

Note: Decentralized decision-making is still a sensitive topic within organizations with a strong waterfall orientation, ITIL processes, strong hierarchies, and command and control structures. But if such companies want to speed up and transform themselves, they need to start the discussion.

Benefit

Purely centralized decision making is a bottleneck in software development and will reduce speed and responsiveness. Further, the taken decisions are often hard to sell to developers because of two reasons: 1) They were not involved, and/ or 2) the results are often not transparent to them. Whenever centralized decisions are taken which directly affect developers, they should be involved in a proper way, so that they understand the reasons.

Especially, in a VUCA world and agile software development, it is hard to foresee the functional, as well as non-functional requirements well. Thus, investing a lot of time in creating generalized and long-lasting concepts is not necessarily the best options for challenges which are volatile and uncertain. Baby-step decisions within the team itself and refactoring of the solution according to the learning can be the better approach.

Bottlenecks, unpredictability, increasing complexity are reasons, why decentralized decision-making is a good alternative to speed up development and relieve the architecture team. They can focus on more strategic or compliance topics.

Example – Spikes and POCs

In agile development a spike could be implemented in one or two iterations to evaluate the best options regarding functional and non-functional requirements. A spike originated from Extreme Programming [10, 98] and is defined as "a task aimed at answering a question or gathering information, rather than at producing shippable product." [21]. The concept of spikes is very similar to what people in the waterfall or business world understand under the term proof of concept: Trying out and evaluating possible solutions.

In the first place trying out different solutions is revealing insights which books or marketing slides are hiding and enable people to experience ups and downs of the solution. More important is, that this approach scales among many teams. Topics to evaluate and decide are given to the teams directly, who come up with proposals. Only the fundamental, strategic decisions are done centralized. Minor decisions are done by the team(s) decentralized.

Further Reading

▷ **Extreme Programming Explained: Embrace Change** [10] by Kent Beck (more on spikes)

 Learn more on decentralized decision making in the video: Greatness (YouTube) by David Marquet (http://bit.ly/2JDn5rp)

6. Simplify

"... it is simplicity that is difficult to make."

(Berthold Brecht)

Simplification comes at two flavors: Functional and technical simplification. Usually, both go hand in hand. With functional simplification we often can also reduce the underlying technical implementation. Simplification is key to fulfill today's challenges. More and more companies are realizing this, and start internal campaigns, e.g., to simplify products and processes to reduce historic grown complexities, which are blocking them to innovate.

I this section you will learn strategies and techniques to simplify solutions. Incremental build solutions need refactoring which will also be discussed in this section.

Contents

6.1. Shake the solution

One not so well-known problem-solving principle is Occam's Razor [114], which states to prefer simplicity. I interpret the principle as following: If you have too many assumptions about the problem to solve, your solution will probably be wrong or lead to an unnecessary complex solution. Assumptions should be reduced (simplified) to come to a good solution.

To get solutions simplified, it often helps to "shake" the solution and look at them from different positions and angles. Try to shape the solution by thinking top-down and again bottom-up. If you have a data-flow or process, then first think left to right and again right to left. Ask questions such as:

▷ Is this all necessary and required?

▷ What if we were living in a perfect technical world? Example: No memory or CPU constraints.

▷ What if we were living in a perfect business world? Example: No complex exceptions or frauds.

▷ What would company X or person Y do? Where X is not your competitor, but one of the FAANG companies[1] (Facebook, Apple, Amazon, Netflix, Google).

▷ How would it look like, if we apply a different principle or pattern? Example: Orchestration vs. Choreography

▷ Is there a new technology which could help us or radically change our approach? Examples: Serverless, In-Memory DB

---

[1] https://en.wikipedia.org/wiki/Facebook,_Apple,_Amazon,_Netflix_and_Google

Benefit

Challenging and shaking the potential solution from different perspective and asking good questions like the above, increases the chance to identify parts of your solution which can be simplified. The answers to the questions may further clarify assumptions and thus lead to a simpler solution with respect to the principle of Occam's razor.

Example – User Interface

Assume, that you have the requirement to enable search for different entities in your company, e.g., employees, customers, contracts, emails, etc. How would you design the user interface? Would it be

▷ one single search box, where you type in your query, like the single search field in google, or

▷ a classical ERP like search dialog with plenty of fields for each attribute and entity, and another set for every connected system which holds similar data?

In my experience, the second approach is often chosen, as "it was always done like this" and "our users are corporate users". Even though, many of those people think that the first solution would be the better approach, they are reluctant. Although they would gain business benefits. And I can only see one reasons why this is: Simplicity is difficult.

What is holding them back?

▷ Technology? Mature search engine technologies exist.

▷ Lacking skills of developers or trust into them? Send them to a training or give them some time to try it out.

▷ Initial investment? Think and calculate mid- or long-term.

There are no real show stoppers. It's probably a mindset problem which you cannot solve by shaking. Still, in this case you found a better solution by simply having a look at google.

6.2. Take a step back

After intense and long architecture or design discussions, highly complex scribbles are often the result. You should never ever see these as the (final) result. Take a step back: Have a look at the big picture again (abstract level). Does it still make sense? Then go through it on the abstract level again and refactor. Sometimes it helps to stop a discussion and continue the next day. At least my brain needs some time to process and to come up with better, more elegant and simpler solutions.

Some actions to force your brain to take a step back, and get to a more abstract thinking mode:

▷ **Ask questions**: What do I want to achieve? What was the exact question or problem statement? Does this option or solution fulfill it?

▷ **Redraw a scribble**: Make boxes around semantic similar items within your scribble. Redraw the boxes onto a new piece of paper. The diagram is now clean and more readable. (And more abstract.) Does this diagram make sense now? Work on it and repeat the cleaning step by grouping items. If the big picture makes sense, then you can dive into the details of each box.

▷ **Use templates**: If you get stuck into details, while creating documents, e.g., decision papers, it helps to use a template. Usually every bigger company has a repository of templates. The template often contains guidance and gives structure. See Section 5.3 for some examples, if you have no template.

▷ **Use frameworks, methods or tools**: For some problems there are already frameworks, methods and tools available, which can be used to analyze, structure and design a solution. Two popular methods are OOAD (Object Oriented Analysis and Design) [113] suited for object oriented programming approaches and DDD (Domain Driven Design) [96] which is a more general approach and often said to work well in the context of microservice architectures.

Benefit

Rushing into a solution too quickly is sometimes working, but more often it's not. Especially, if the topic is complex. Step back, in the sense of looking at a more abstract level, helps you to identify whether the solution fits into the overall picture.

Taking some time, especially overnight, is very helpful. Studies have identified that human brains consolidate and optimize information, gathered on the day, during sleep [22]. That means, if you get stuck while working out options and possible solutions, continue later or better, the next day.

Anecdotal, people often tell that they had a problem which they could not solve during the day, but after some sleep, they suddenly had a great idea to partially or even completely solve the problem. Studies indicate that this is working. People were given a task (training) and afterwards divided into two groups: One with 8 hours of sleep after training, and the other group with no sleep until the retest was done. "More than twice as many subjects gained insight into the hidden rule after sleep as after wakefulness, regardless of time of day." [87] What's not working is to omit the initial task (training) and only sleep. Thus, you need to first think about the problem.

Important: I need to get you back on the ground, before you continue reading. This method is obviously not a silver bullet. It is not enough to start thinking a bit about the problem, go to sleep, and have the solution the next day. Hard work is required: Thinking, brainstorming, scribbling, controversial discussions, reading books, etc. But sleeping can support the problem solving.

Example – 2 Day Workshop

If you have tough decisions to make, or find out how to improve, innovate, etc, a good idea is to split a workshop into two days. One of the many advantages is to have a bit of time and sleep to think about the discussed topics. But keep it time-boxed, otherwise you will never come to a result.

6.3. Divide and Conquer

A popular method in computer science to solve complex algorithmic problems is to (recursively) break down a complex problem into smaller sub-problems of the same or related type, until these become simple enough to be solved directly [95]. If the problems are broken down properly, the solution of the sub-problems can be solved individually, and together, the sub-solutions are the solution for the whole. Figure 6.1 illustrates this approach.

Crucial to this approach is to validate at the end, that the small pieces really fit and work together well. For that, take a step back and check the overall picture again on a more abstract level.

Benefit

Sub-problems are usually easier to solve as they narrow down the solution space and the number of assumptions. Furthermore, for sub-problems you may identify patterns and anti-patterns easier.

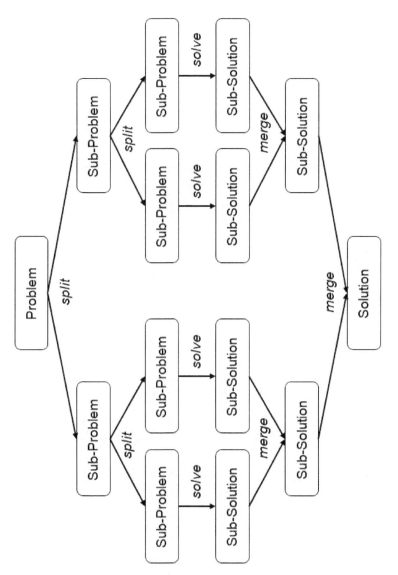

Figure 6.1.: Divide and Conquer

It can also have a huge impact on performance when applied. For example, Quicksort [116] one of the fasted sorting algorithms, is using divide and conquer. Another application of divide and conquer is MapReduce [107] to process large amounts of data with a parallel and distributed algorithm on a cluster.

Example – OOAD

Have you ever wondered why architects are drawing so many diagrams? It's not only to visualize problems and communicate solutions. But they are also helping to break down complex problems (big boxes) into simpler sub-problems (smaller boxes).

Within the object-oriented programming (OOP) space, a well-known technique is used to analyze and design software applications, systems and even the business itself. It's called Object Oriented Analysis and Design (OOAD) [113]. This technique utilizes UML as modeling language.

Within OOAD, divide and conquer starts already during the analysis of the problem, where objects and their relationship are identified [113]. Assume you want to build the software for an ATM. The first step is to identify the real-world objects which are interacting with the system, e.g., customer, bank, account, money. Then you identify the behavior (process) and states (data) of these objects. Based on this you can derive different models, to better understand and design the future systems, e.g., class and component diagrams for structure and activity and use-case diagrams for behavior. With this approach, the real-world is divided and conquered.

Example – Microservices

Breaking down monoliths into a system of systems a.k.a. microservices, is a form of problem solving, too. Sub-components are created, which are specialist in solving specific problems. The effort and complexity are to build the system in a way that the sub-systems are working together properly.

Example – Layers

Architects love to use layers to break down problems. To inspire you, I have created a small list of layers, required for a random application:

▷ Infrastructure and Services, e.g., servers, DBs, external service providers.

▷ Application and Tools, i.e., the developed system itself and the development tools.

▷ Data, e.g., test data, quality, migration, interfaces.

▷ Security, e.g., authentication, authorization, access.

▷ User, e.g., ergonomic, documentation, training.

▷ Change & Release, e.g., how to handle new Features and bug-fixes.

6.4. Refactoring is not evil

In the past I have experienced a resistance to refactor code, tests or architecture. And there are plenty of reasons for it, foremost lack of time. Unfortunately, and this is independent from the development method you apply, your solution will get increasingly difficult to enhance and maintain, until you have the feeling that a complete rebuild is necessary. It's pretty natural that applications and systems are growing in complexity, if the right measures are not in place or are not applied properly. One measure is refactoring to restructure and simplify the solution.

Many scientists have studied the evolution of software and its related attributes over time, and they came up with some laws: One prominent set of laws are "Lehman's laws of software evolution" [105]. In this context I would like to highlight the first two of them (according to [31]):

▷ **Continuing change** – A software will become progressively less satisfying to its users over time, unless it is continually adapted to meet new needs.

▷ **Increasing complexity** — A software system will become progressively more complex over time, unless explicit work is done to reduce its complexity.

There are three prominent types of refactoring (according to [85]):

▷ **Code refactoring**: This is most often understood under the term refactoring. It's the refactoring of program source code.

▷ **Database refactoring**: Changing the database schema, which improves its design and related quality characteristics while retaining both its behavioral and informational semantics.

▷ **User interface (UI) refactoring**: Changing the UI while retaining its semantics, to e.g., improve the user experience.

As an architect it is part of your job to have an eye on the complexity of the code base. If no refactoring measures are applied, the maintainability of the application will become hard. Adding new features will take longer and may introduce new bugs more easily.

Beside these more code related refactoring topics, there are also architectural refactoring options, like:

▷ **Monolith to microservice architecture**: Transforming a classic monolith architecture to a more modern microservice oriented architecture. This can be for example achieved using the

Strangler Pattern [26]: Modules or components of the Monolith are extracted one after another and operated as microservices.

▷ **Infrastructure changes**: Refactoring the application, so that it can be operated within a different infrastructure. For example, porting the application from Windows to Unix, or in more complex cases, porting from a mainframe system to AWS.

These more high-level refactoring approaches are related to overarching strategies. One does not simply refactor an application or system landscape to a microservice oriented architecture. Good reasons and good strategies are required, before doing such a drastic change.

Benefit

There are many people and books who claim that refactoring is highly beneficial [49, 28, 85]. If you do not want to rework or even throw away your system after a short period of time, you better consider refactoring as necessary to keep up with key quality attributes.

Unfortunately, I have experienced in the past, that (especially) management rejects refactoring, because of various reasons. Although studies indicate that refactoring is valuable, people are struggling with explaining and justifying it to management and customers without having a concrete business need [85]. This is probably one reason, why refactoring is often done as a side exercise while implementing new features.

I believe that refactoring is not evil. Especially, within agile software development it is inevitable to continuously refactor the incrementally build software, to enable further extendability, maintenance, etc. "Refactoring improves the design of software, makes software easier to understand, helps to find bugs and also helps in executing the program faster. [...] It changes the way a developer thinks about the implementation when refactoring." [85]

If refactoring is done regularly, it is fine to start with a more complex solution, and later rethink and simplify the solution, after key insights have been made.

Before you can recommend refactoring, keep in mind to have the following in place:

> ▷ Enough automated tests, which can ensure the proper functionality of the system after refactoring.

> ▷ Buy-in from your stakeholders, otherwise they may ask, why your delivery speed is decreasing.

Example – Red-Green-Refactor

Within the domain of test-driven development (TDD) refactoring is so to say "build-in". You start by writing the first test case, even before the first line of code has been written. Then the test case is executed and, of course, it's failing (red). The code is enhanced and fixed until the test passes (green). Then the code is optimized by refactoring, e.g., by eliminating redundancies, simplifications, etc. Tests need to stay green after refactoring.

Next is to add a second test case for the next requirement. The test is executed and it's red. The code is fixed until both test cases are green. Refactoring is applied. This exercise is repeated until all functional and non-functional acceptance criteria are covered as test cases and all are green. This approach is called Red-Green-Refactor [53]. Compare with Figure 6.2

TDD is not only continuously testing code intensively while (and even before) implementation, but also a strategy to find a solution to (complex) problems. Instead of a top-down approach, where you first draft the solution in form of a concept, this approach is bottom-up. The solution is created incrementally with small steps. As testing

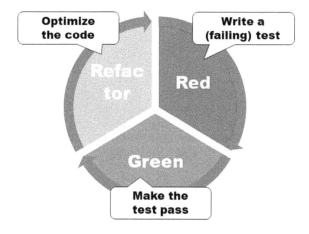

Figure 6.2.: Red-green refactoring

and refactoring is build-in, the promise is to create high quality code in the end.

Further Reading

▷ **Refactoring. Improving the Design of Existing Code** [28] by Martin Fowler

▷ **Clean code: a handbook of agile software craftsmanship** [52] by Robert C. Martin

7. Code

> *"Any fool can write code that a computer can understand. Good programmers write code that humans can understand."*
>
> *(Martin Fowler)*

Even as an (IT) Enterprise Architect, the most abstract level of architecture, and usually with a business focus, you should still know what developers are doing. This is especially true for architects who work more closer with developers. If you do not understand developer's challenges well enough, you may face two major problems:

▷ Developers won't accept your sayings, as they directly know, that you have no clue.

▷ You do not understand the needs of developers to lead a successful project or product development.

In this section you will learn how to increase your coding skills by having a side project, trying out new things and learning more about clean code.

Contents

7.1. Have a side project

The purpose of this is to try out new technologies and tools, to find out how development could be done today and in the future. Reading a tutorial or some pros and cons is good. But this is just "book knowledge". Hands-on-experience is better.

With side projects you make new experiences. Experience is the combination of observations, emotions and hypothesis [76]. While trying out something new, you observe how the build solution behaves. Some things will work out, other won't. This will trigger emotions: You will be satisfied by a cool new feature or get frustrated with the low maturity of a new framework. Finally, you will state a hypothesis, e.g., framework x is not mature enough, we should not use it now. And as it was frustrating, you will remember it better.

Benefit

Experience is key. And with side-projects you can easily build up experience. This will help you to take better decisions in your day to day work or for more future directed, strategic decisions.

As I started programming I had no code completion and only some utility libraries to speed up development. Younger people laugh at me, when I tell them about that time. But, that was reality in my first corporate project after university: SAP with no code completion. And mainly duplicated code everywhere, because it was too time consuming to extract code for reuse, as no refactoring support is included as we know it from today's IDEs like Eclipse.

Today, you have tons of programming languages, frameworks, tools, processes and practices. Only if you made some experiences and have a rough overview on the major trends, you can take part of the conversation and steer development into the right direction to solve problems in the most efficient and future oriented way.

66

Another benefit of side projects, if taken seriously, is that you can experience the complete life-cycle. Starting from defining requirements, over implementing, testing and deploying, and finally maintaining the app. And, if things work out well, you need to scale to handle the increasing number of users. You can learn much about the interplay of each phase, especially the impact of design decisions on maintenance.

Example – GitLab + Firebase + Angular

The latest advances in technology are fascinating as less setup is required to start a side-project and all for free. No hassle to order and configure a server anymore or to worry about its maintenance to stay up to date with security fixes. Try out the latest technology with an infrastructure which many corporate companies are dreaming of. To highlight some which you get with Firebase and GitLab for example:

▷ High scalability and performance

▷ Hosting and storing with content delivery networks (CDNs)

▷ Build-in authentication (social login), monitoring and analytics

▷ Production ready machine learning capabilities for common use cases

▷ Real-time databases

▷ Maintenance free tools, like source code management, bug-tracker, wiki, continuous integration and continuous deployment (CI/CD) capabilities for automated build, test and deployment

Give it a try and experiment with what is possible today. To kick-start your side-project, you can for example use Angular, GitLab and Firebase. With this setup, you can even easily build a CI/CD pipeline to automate all tedious work, such as build, test and deployment as depicted in Figure 7.1. Locally, you only need to install node.js, git and a development environment such as Visual Studio Code.

For this kind of setup, there are thousands of tutorials available. Even I created one:

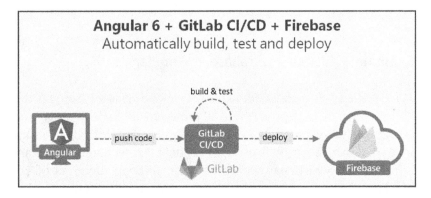

Figure 7.1.: Exemplary setup for a side-project

CI/CD with Angular 6 & Firebase & GitLab [62] (http://bit.ly/2PQaNMH)

7.2. Find the right things to try out

You cannot try out everything. This is simply impossible. You need a structured approach. One source I recently discovered is the Technology Radar [83] from ThoughtWorks. They categorize technologies, tools, platforms, languages and frameworks into four categories:

Figure 7.2.: Zalando's technology radar

▷ **Adopt**: "strong feeling to be ready for enterprise usage"

▷ **Trial**: "enterprise should try it in one project that can handle the risk"

▷ **Assess**: "explore how it affects your enterprise"

▷ **Hold**: "process with caution"

You could also create your very own technology radar for your company. Zalando, a retailer, maintains a similar Technology Radar [129] for their company and open sourced the tool, to create radars like in Figure 7.2. They categorize frameworks, data management, languages and infrastructure into the above-mentioned categories.

Benefit

With the categorization of the Technology Radar it is easier to get an overview of new things and their readiness to better evaluate which trend to explore next.

Finding the right project to work on is obviously important. But, more important for private projects is, that you are motivated to execute them. Otherwise, you are less likely to do it. You will get frustrated and will not learn anything. Even the hottest technology is the wrong for you, if you have a strong aversion to it.

Example — Raspberry PI

A friend of mine has always been interested in playing with hardware. This was something I always disliked. I wanted to program software. But then the Rasbperry PI was released, and this small piece of hardware got me. It was highly motivating for me to play around with it and I had some great learning.

This was the opener to hardware programming for me. Before, I tried it here and there, but was so frustrated, that I just not continued and stopped exploring.

Further Reading

Technology Radar [83] by ThoughtWorks
(https://thght.works/2H5elYV)

Technology Radar [129] by Zalando
(https://zln.do/2H25dEm)

7.3. Clean Code

Understanding how good code looks like and what can potentially go wrong during coding is a good trait every architect should have. Of course, it depends on the architecture level you are working on and the development methodology you apply, how much code you see and write in your day to day work.

"Code is clean if it can be understood easily – by everyone on the team. With understandability comes readability, changeability, extensibility and maintainability. All the things needed to keep a project going over a long time without accumulating up a large amount of technical debt." [8]

Benefit

Depending on which level you are doing architecture, you will see code more or less often. And distinguishing good from bad code is a powerful tool. You can use it retrospectively to assess the quality of the overall product with respect to the likelihood of containing defects, or the overall maintainability. On the other hand, you can guide developers to write good code, to increase the quality.

"Most software defects are introduced when changing existing code." [8] One reason is, that developers cannot grasp the change effects fully. Applying clean code techniques, the code is easier to understand and minimizes the risk of introducing errors.

Having clean code in place is also good for on-boarding new developers and easier while debugging. If you directly understand the code, you can use the saved time for actual development.

Example

Some simple examples of dirty and clean code can be found in Table 7.1 in pseudo code. I hope, that you see the difference, and how clean code enables understandably of code. Especially, the last example about inline code comments is remarkable, when it comes to the fight: do we need code comments or not. I think, a method and its parameters should be commented. Additional comments should be included only in a few exceptional cases. The code itself should be understandable without additional comments.

If you want to learn how clean code looks like, then I recommend to have a look at the programming language Smalltalk and some code of it. This is a great resource to learn and understand how good code could look like.

Further Reading

> **Clean code: a handbook of agile software craftsmanship** [52] by Robert C. Martin

> **Clean architecture: a craftsman's guide to software structure and design**[54], by Robert C. Martin

 Clean Code Cheat Sheet by bbv software services [8] (http://bit.ly/2H0FYCa)

Type	Dirty Code

Names of variables and methods	`// dirty`
	`var cmnt;`
	
	`// clean`
	`var comment;`

Show intention	`// dirty`
	`if ('paid' ==`
	`transaction.status())`
	
	`// clean`
	`if (transaction.isPaid())`

Use verbs and nouns properly for methods	`// dirty`
	`amountStock()`
	
	`// clean`
	`getStockAmount()`

Don't hard code	`// dirty`
	`if(day == '1') { ... }`
	
	`// clean`
	`if(day == DAYS.MONDAY) { ... }`

Don't comment bad code, rewrite it	`// dirty`
	`// transaction is due`
	`if(a=='1' AND b == '2'`
	`    OR c == '3')`
	
	`// clean`
	`if(transaction.isDue())`

Table 7.1.: Comparison of dirty and clean code

8. Document

> *"Meaningful architecture is a living, vibrant process of deliberation, design, & decision, not just documentation."*
>
> *(Grady Booch)*

Architectural documentation is sometimes more and sometimes less important. Important documents are for example architectural decisions or code guidelines. Initial documentation is often helpful before coding starts and need to be refined continuously. Other documentation can be automatically generated. And code itself is also a form of documentation.

In this section you will learn more about documentation and how to avoid tedious, manual work to create and keep documentation up-to-date, by generating documentation using models. Further, you will learn more about what to document and to which extend. Finally, a quick overview of architecture frameworks is given, to provide you with templates and ideas on what and how to document.

Contents

8.1. Clean Code – Revisited

Code is the best documentation if written with good intention. A good architect should be capable to distinguish between good and bad code as mentioned in Section 7.3. Clean code is one approach to increase the value of code with respect to documentation.

Another good approach is to stick as close to the common code conventions and guidelines of the used language or framework. Specific naming and coding conventions, folder structures, or code organization are some examples.

Benefit

If code is written well, no extensive additional documentation is necessary. You can understand the code by reading it. This saves a lot of time as less documentation needs to be written and it's easier to regularly update it, which is even more time consuming and error prone.

By complying to language and framework conventions, other developers will have it easier to understand the code. Especially, when working together with many people, this is a huge benefit. No cumbersome documentation needs to be read beforehand. Productive work can start as soon as the development environment is setup.

Example – Angular Style Guide

A good example is the Angular Style Guide [4] which defines how an Angular application should look like. It defines naming conventions, file structures, application structures and many things more. This lowers the learning curve a new developer needs to work with the code. And it gives the code a consistency which eases understanding

```
  1   a-c|
  2        □ a-component                                    User Snippet
             Angular component snippet                              ⊕
             □ a-component-root
      - - - - - - - - - - - - - - - - - - - - - - - - - - - - - - - -
      import { Component, OnInit } from '@angular/core';

  3   @Component({
  4       moduleId: module.id,
  5       selector: 'selector',
  6       templateUrl: 'feature.component.html'
  7   })
  8   export class FeatureComponent implements OnInit {
  9       constructor() { }
 10
 11       ngOnInit() { }
 12   }
 13
```

Figure 8.1.: Code snippet with Angular.

and maintenance of the code. If, for example, you encounter a variable named variable$, you instantly know, that it is an Observable, and the variable without the dollar sign stores the most recent value.

Additionally, the style guide defines principles how to apply the framework. For example, it explains when to use directives or services and how they should be implemented, so that it fits into the overall architecture. This consistency eases the usage of the build application. Developers know what they get and what to expect from code they may not have written by themselves.

Another great advice within the Angular documentation is to use snippets or templates as depicted in Figure 8.1. If you want to create a component, you start typing "a-component" and the IDE suggests inserting the template. File templates or snippets help following consistent styles and patterns. Alternatively, Angular provides a CLI (command line interface) to generate code templates on demand.

8.2. Generate documentation whenever possible

Systems are changing quickly, and it is hard to update the documentation continuously. Whether it is about APIs or system landscapes in form of Configuration Management DBs (CMDB): The underlying information often changes too fast to keep the corresponding documentation up to date by hand.

One solution to ever changing information is to automatically generate the latest documentation based on the underlying code, infrastructure, models, etc. This way, you always have the latest and most accurate documentation possible.

Benefit

Keeping documentation and actual implementation in sync is cumbersome. Hence, you can save a lot of time to generate documentation based on the actual implementation. Using specification documents is also not ideal, as requirements change, and let's be honest, specifications are rarely implemented as they were written.

Note: If you apply model driven development, you can derive the documentation easily from the models itself. Additionally, you can auto-generate code and test skeletons to kick-start your development, or to set some fixed boundaries for all developers. More on this in Section 8.3

Example – API Documentation

For APIs you can auto generate documentation based on the definition file, if you are model driven, or directly from the source code

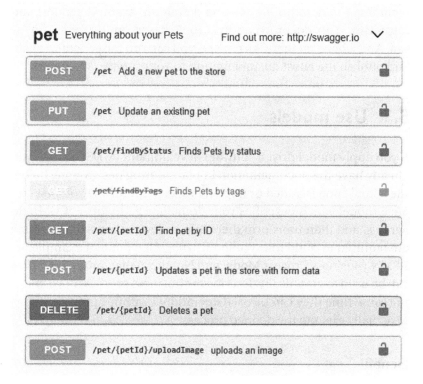

Figure 8.2.: API documentation with swagger

itself. A lot of tools exist for that purpose: Two popular options are Swagger [79] and RAML [70].

In Figure 8.2 an exemplary swagger `.html` documentation is depicted. For every resource a list of possible HTTP requests and URIs is shown. Every item can be expanded, which opens the details, including the description, schema definition, example request and responses. This documentation is 100% based on the model file itself. And whenever there is a change, you can run the generator again and publish the latest documentation to your service consumers.

8.3. Use models

If you apply model driven software development (MDSD) [108], you already have the documentation in place during design time, before the actual code is added or implemented. With MDSD you first create a model which describes your domain, e.g., in form of UML diagrams, and then transform them into code or other artifacts which are required to build the system [27, 108]. One popular example are BPMN (Business Process Model and Notation) diagrams [106]. They can be used to graphically describe the business process (flow) and at the same time they can be used operational within a process engine to actually execute the defined process.

Benefit

In contrast to generating the documentation from the actual implementation, you start with the documentation and derive the skeleton for implementation from it. This can save time during implementation as the model can be used in best case to generate the framework, into which the business logic is added in the right place. Further, it helps to reduce manually induced errors. Template code is usually better tested than hand written code.

More general advantages of MDSD in this context are (based on [68]):

▷ **Increased developer productivity**: Code or documentation is generated.

▷ **Increased communication**: Models are free of implementation details which eases understanding and communication with business people.

▷ **Consistency**: Generated artifacts are consistent among each other. Changes are applied in one place only. Architecture decisions can be enforced.

▷ **Repeatability**: Proofed and tested generators can be applied in other projects, which increases the return on investment.

▷ **Capture of domain knowledge**: Models use business terms. And the patterns and transformation logic, written by experts, is conserved to realize the business specifics within the system in the generator.

Note: MDSD has been discussed controversial in the past. And I am not promoting or demoting MDSD. You need to carefully evaluate in which areas MDSD makes sense and where not. Some disadvantages according to [68] and from my own experience are:

▷ Workarounds may be necessary to make the generated artifacts work as expected.

▷ Models getting complex and are hard to maintain.

▷ Time to generate models can explode and rather decrease development speed.

▷ Generators are not supporting the domain specific circumstances and need to be adapted.

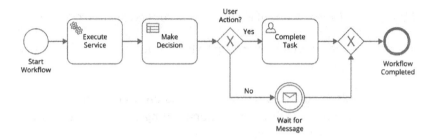

Figure 8.3.: Sample BPMN diagram, fully executable (Source: Camunda Documentation)

Example – BPMN

If you want to automate business processes by orchestrating different tasks, e.g., calling web services, integrating APIs, making decisions, and from time to time integrate a human worker, then you should have a look at BPMN in combination with a (light-weight) process engine like camunda [16], Activiti [1] or ActiveVOS [42].

Business analysts and developers can design the process with the standardized BPMN 2.0 language in close collaboration and focus on the business context. The language is visual and easy to learn. The BPMN process itself can then be executed by the process engine, after the developer has added meta information on the model, e.g., which variables should be used on a gateway or which java class should be invoked for specific tasks.

In my experience, using BPMN in combination with a proper (light-weight) process engine, is a powerful combination, as it brings together business and IT. Instead of transforming requirement documents many times, e.g., word, powerpoint, visio, UML and finally code, they can directly collaborate and understand each other using one diagram.

To achieve best results you should follow defined design guidelines.

To get you started here are two resources:

 BPMN Modeling Guidelines **by Signavio** [78]
(http://bit.ly/2WnQade)

Best practices for creating BPMN 2.0 process diagrams **by camunda** [15]
(http://bit.ly/2Y1p3oS)

8.4. As much as necessary, as little as possible

The purpose of documentation is, that it is used and read. Hence, keep in mind the reader of your documentation. Keep it short, crisp and clean. Include as much information as necessary, but omit, or hide, the tiny details somewhere else, e.g., in a later paragraph or in the appendix.

Try to focus on the one major thing and include only the necessary information for this one thing. Especially, for decision papers it is more important to tell a convincing story instead of throwing tons of arguments or numbers. If you have 20 options, narrow them down to the best 3 to 5. And only discuss these. Put the other thoughts somewhere else and simply say, that they have been evaluated (long list), but are not good enough for being short-listed.

Have a look at documentation you or your co-workers have created in the past (source code, models, decision papers, etc.) and ask yourself the following questions:

▷ Is all necessary information included to understand it?

▷ Which information are really required, and which could be omitted?

▷ Does the document have a red line?

Benefit

Focusing on one major topic at a time helps to establish a red line. It will be easier for the reader to understand the message. If further information is required, the reader can look it up in another section. Otherwise, the reader may be overwhelmed by the information and does not get the point at all. Hence, less is more.

By reflecting on activities from the past, you can learn to get better. Grab some documents from the past and read them. If you do not understand the documentation, then obviously something is missing. What is missing? What is unclear? By doing this exercise, you can also enhance the document directly, if the documentation is still required. Apply the Boy Scout rule from clean code: Leave the code (in this case the documentation) better than found it [52]. While learning, you can directly enhance documentation.

Note: A much as necessary, as little as possible is a universal advice to all kind of software architecture challenges.

Example – Templates

If a specific documentation needs to be created several times, e.g., decision papers, code comments or commit messages, you should create a template with a clear structure and instruction or placeholder text. This will guide you to put the right information in the right place. A red line can be established. Past learning can be used to enhance and shape the template continuously.

You can directly try out to standardize your git commit message by creating a ~/.gitmessage template. Git commit messages are probably the best documentation of the evolution of your code base. "A good commit message should tell the reader, why the change was necessary, how the change addresses that need, and any side-effects the change will introduce." [35]

8.5. Learn more about architecture frameworks

This action could be categorized under many other sections of this book as well. I put it here, as architecture frameworks are providing "tools" which feel heavy on the documentation site. Although their added value is not limited to documentation at all.

Two popular enterprise architecture frameworks which are often mentioned are the following:

▷ **TOGAF: The Open Group Architecture Framework** [33, 122]

▷ **Zachmann Framework** [5, 126]

Benefit

Learning or even getting certified in such framework teaches you to tackle architecture more systematically. They typically consist of the following three components to support the systematical architecture work and bootstrap architecture work if no proper one is in place yet (based on [97]):

▷ **Description advice**: Architecture Artifacts Map or Viewpoint

▷ **Library Process advice**: Architecture Development Method, with supporting guidance.

▷ **Organization advice:** EA Governance Model and more

In the context of documentation, especially, the architecture artifact templates are a good resource to use and adapt to your needs. Enterprise architecture feels heavy on the documentation side, as it also includes a governance framework with maturity models and metrics to effectively steer and communicate architecture with objective numbers.

Note: These kind of frameworks can be helpful resources for architecture artifact templates, processes and good practices. I am convinced that adopting practices from such frameworks bring value to the enterprise. But there are also critical voices which needs to be mentioned, e.g., that TOGAF "is based on a methodology previously rejected as ineffective (TAFIM[1])" or "it claims to be based on best practice but is unable to provide any examples of successful implementation" [45].

Example – Architecture Artifacts

Architecture frameworks like TOGAF provide process descriptions, templates and artifacts. But there is another resource for artifacts and templates, not only for architecture, I would like to share with you. One nearly forgotten software development approach is the Rational Unified Process (RUP) [117, 46]. It is an iterative software development framework and comes with an extensive set of resources, such as templates, concepts, guidelines, checklists, and many more.

Note: The RUP documentation was not updated since years and some items appear to be outdated. Still, I believe that this collection is a good resource for inspiration.

---

[1] Technical Architecture Framework for Information Management

Link to Templates

Software Architecture Templates within RUP
[40] (http://bit.ly/2H1rtOs)

Software Architecture Templates within TOGAF
[33] (registration required,
http://bit.ly/2HsPHjZ)

9. Communicate

"The art of communication is the language of leadership."

(James Humes)

From my observations, communication is one of the most underestimated skill. If you are brilliant in design but cannot communicate your ideas, your thoughts are likely to have less impact or even fail to succeed. Architects are often facilitators of meetings, bridging the gap between people with different background and viewpoints, i.e., business and IT.

In this section you will learn communication facilitation techniques which lead to better meeting and workshop outcomes. You will learn to be more transparent, have the right information for the right people in the right time and to give talks to a larger audience.

Contents

9.1. Learn how to communicate and facilitate

As an architect you often do not only participate in meetings, but you facilitate, moderate or drive the meeting. Communication and facilitation techniques help you to get the most benefit out of it.

Good meetings within the architecture area are often coined by discussions with different people having different point of views, with the common goal of finding a solution for a given problem. Because of the complexity of architecture topics and the broad solution space, there is often not an obvious solution. It's not a "business as usual" meeting where everything is clear.

Ideal architecture discussions follow the following sequence: Options are generated, discussed, evaluated and finally summarized and decided. Unfortunately, this model of decision making is not realistic. Discussions may get stuck after a specific point and people feel frustrated and get angry. This phenomenon was also identified and described in literature. Hence, according to Kaner [44] a group goes through three phases of decision making as depicted in Figure 9.1:

▷ **Divergent Zone**: Different options are generated; diverse viewpoints are exchanged and a free-flowing open discussion is happening. →Solution space expands.

▷ **Groan Zone**: Group members integrate different options and views with their own by sifting through them and discussing some in-depth. →Critical Phase.

▷ **Convergent Zone**: Options are evaluated, ideas are categorized, and key points are summarized to conclude with excising judgment. →Solution space narrows down to final solution.

Facilitation within the divergent and convergent zones is straight forward. For example, you could apply brainstorming techniques to

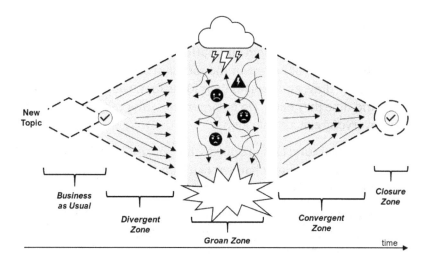

Figure 9.1.: Dynamics of group decisions

generate ideas and dot voting to pick the preferred solution by the group at the end. Within both zones, I fell that people are motivated to work. But the groan zone needs attention. If this phase is not facilitated properly, the meeting may explode, and no outcome will be generated.

Group members struggle to integrate unfamiliar or opposing views, options and ideas and different ways of thinking with their own. Discussions heat up and group members may become repetitive, defensive, insensitive, aggressive, etc. The role of the facilitator is to detect it and give group members space and structure.

My facilitation tips are the following:

▷ **Set the stage**: State the purpose and outcome, so that everyone agrees. Make sure that everyone who is required attends the meeting. Describe and agree on the process to come to a decision. Especially, who and how the decision is taken: Team vs. Individual person or consensus vs. majority. Agree on communication rules.

▷ **Visualize the problem and options**: Use a white board or flip-chart to get all people in the room on the same page. Let everyone draw and explain their ideas first. Give them the space and time they need. Do not interrupt. After they have finished, everyone can ask questions.

▷ **Give structure**: Group options into "boxes" based on identified criteria. Draw flow charts or fish-bone diagrams. Do a benefit-effort-analysis as described in the example below.

▷ **Ask questions**: Use the "5 Whys" technique to find out the root cause of a problem. From anecdotal observations, 5 question-answer iterations are enough to resolve the problem. [90]

▷ **Set a time-box**: Stop endless discussion without results. This can be achieved by setting clear time-boxes. And really stop after the time is up.

▷ **Parking lot**: Put topics aside on the parking lot, to re-focus. It is easy to deviate from the topic or overstretch the time. Put them aside and discuss them later or in a follow up. Focus is key.

These techniques may sound simple, but they are hard to master. Try them out, and make your own experience. Use your instincts and pay attention to the mood of every individual.

Benefit

Understanding the dynamics of group decisions, and how to manage them properly, is a powerful and required tool not only for architects. If not done properly, you may get stuck in the groan zone without any outcome. People are fighting against each other and the longer it takes, the less likely it becomes to solve the conflict. You probably have experienced such situations in the past, that after some unsuccessful meetings escalations to upper management are happening, which lead to thoughtless decisions, just to have a solution. In the end, most are dissatisfied, and the overall quality suffers.

"Misunderstanding and miscommunication are normal, natural aspects of participatory decision-making. The Groan Zone is a direct, inevitable consequence of the diversity that exists in any group." [44] Thus, you do not need to worry about it, instead, acknowledge that this phase exists. Groups that overcome the stressful groan zone, are more likely to discover common ground, which is a precondition for insightful and innovative co-thinking.

Example – Benefit / Effort Analysis

A simple and structured visualization technique for decision making is to lay out options according to their potential benefit and effort in a grid as depicted in Figure 9.2. Options with low benefit and high effort should be avoided, whereas options with high benefit and low effort are quick wins or low hanging fruits. Options with high benefit and high effort require strategic planning.

This technique is obviously not rocket science. But by applying the technique it visualizes options and triggers valuable conversations and discussions easier. And it gives a structure and overview of the discussed options.

Further Reading

▷ **Facilitator's guide to participatory decision-making** [44] by Sam Kaner

▷ **UZMO - Thinking With Your Pen** [36] by Martin Haussmann

Figure 9.2.: Visualize options in benefit-effort grid

9.2. Be comfortable with talking to larger groups

Presenting your ideas to small or large groups should be doable for you. If you feel uncomfortable with this, start presenting to your best friend. Enlarge the group slowly. This is something which you can only learn by doing and by leaving your personal comfort zone. Be patient with yourself, this process may take some time.

I assume that people with a technical background have problems with speaking to larger groups. If you are not affected, feel free to skip this section.

Some of my personal tips which make me comfortable speaking to a larger group are the following:

> ▷ **Know the content by heart.** If you feel uncomfortable, your brain is busy with fighting anxiety. Hence, knowing what you want to say is crucial.

▷ **Get the first three sentences right.** After the first three sentences the initial nervousness usually drops.

▷ **Establish a personal connection.** Know your audience. Talk to people before you enter the stage. If you know the people, it is usually easier.

Note: I think that tips like doing meditation or thinking of a naked audience are not helpful at all. The only thing which helps in the long run is experience. Hence, leave your comfort zone and try it out. My first talks were horrible. But I am thankful for the experience, as I could learn a lot from them, also about myself.

Benefit

Being able to give talks to larger groups is important for architects. At some point in your career, you want to take care of the architecture for a couple of teams, projects, products, or the entire company. This requires you to give strategy and vision talks to a broad audience, including developers, managers and C-level.

Being comfortable with larger groups eases to deliver key messages. Nervousness and anxiety may hinder this. Having routines and experience gives you the required security.

Even if you have a lot of experience in giving speeches, and you do not even need to prepare yourself anymore, there will be this one speech, which will be different: A very important person is sitting in the audience, you need to use a different language, or you are sick. Then you hopefully remember the tips from above or have already your own routine to get yourself into "the speech" mode.

Example – Expand your comfort zone with baby steps

Going out of your comfort zone is necessary to adapt to new situations and being able to give a talk to large groups. Figure 9.3 il-

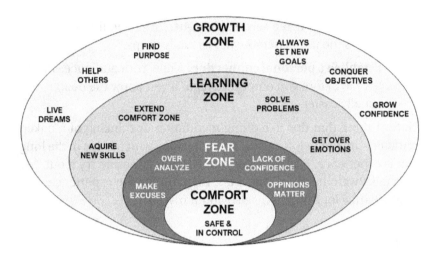

Figure 9.3.: Expand your comfort zone

lustrates the zones in which we live and work.[1] In order to learn and grow, you first need to overcome the "fear zone". Intuitively, you know how to overcome this zone, otherwise, you would not be able to learn new skills or solve problems. Unfortunately, for different topics the fear zone can vary in size, e.g., giving public speeches. Still, you need to overcome it to learn and grow.

But taking too big steps comes at a risk, and you may hurt yourself psychological or even physical. Hence, I suggest taking baby steps.

As a beginner start with the following in the next meetings:

▷ Introduce team members with each other or the agenda

▷ Give a 5min project update to your colleagues

You just need some practice. And the above situations are of low risk. More advanced steps are then:

---

[1]I first saw a similar illustration in a blog post [81]

▷ Give a talk to a small group, together with a colleague, e.g., about the next steps and open problems

▷ Give a talk to a small group on your own

▷ Facilitate a decision meeting with well-known peers

You see the pattern? Expanding your comfort zone with baby steps. As depicted in Figure 9.3: Whenever you leave your comfort zone, and make it to the learning zone, you can actually grow your comfort zone. You acquire new insights or skills and get over your emotions of fear or embarrassment. You learn or even get used to new situations which, naturally, become part of your comfort zone.

9.3. Find the right level of communication

Different stakeholders have different interests and views. They need to be addressed individually on their level. Before you communicate, check if the information you want to share against the criteria in Table 9.1. As discussed earlier, organizations have hierarchies which need to be addressed in communication. For example, a developer is interested in details, whereas a manager wants to have a summary. The example below explains the table in more details.

Benefit

It is highly frustrating for you and the stakeholder you approach, if the level of communication does not match. People expect to be approached in a specific way. And architects, as mentioned several times before, need to bridge the gap between different stakeholders. No one else will do it.

Having the ability to speak with everyone within an organization, from developer to the board members, was also described by Gregor Hohpe [38, 37]. He describes it as an architect elevator, where

	Level in Hierarchy	
	Low	**High**
Details	Detailed	Summarized
Source	Internal	External
Time Scale	Current	Forward Looking
Scope	Narrow	Wide
Language	Technical	Business
Goal	Get things done	Increase ROI
Frequency	High	Low

Table 9.1.: Differences in communication based on hierarchical level

architects are connecting the "engine room" in the basement with the "penthouse". People in the penthouse "feel disconnected from the reality in their organization and confused by the rapid technical advancements. They are therefore grateful if someone reaches out to them, speaks their language, but also has their feet firmly planted in the engine room." [38] He concludes to use the elevator more often.

Example – Developer vs. Manager

Based on Table 9.1, a developer is usually interested in the details of the solution. The scope of the discussion is just to understand the solution to get things done now. The information is based on internal discussions and reflects the current work. On the other hand, a manager or board member, wants to have a summary and is interested in the future. How are others, outside of the company are tackling the problem and how does it help to achieve the goals, e.g., cost reduction or generating new customers. Which effects does the decision have on other projects or products?

You see, based on the same, underlying decision, the communication looks completely different. In practice, it is even worse, as different people have different interests and communication demands. You can have a manager who wants to know the technical details. And sometimes the manager is not even interested in the details but wants to challenge you by asking.

9.4. Communicate often

A brilliant architecture is worthless if nobody knows about it. Distribute, show and tell your ideas, visions and target architecture, regularly and on every level within your organization. Schedule meetings with developers, architects and managers to show them the requested, desired or defined way.

Direct communication is important as well as asynchronous communication. Write internal blog posts, publish in your wiki or send updates via mail. You cannot and maybe do not want to talk to everyone but keeping them informed.

Of course, there are people within your organization who need to be updated more frequently than others. This goes back to the right level of communication, described in the previous Section 9.3. For example, a developer needs to be involved more often than a board member.

Benefit

Keeping all stakeholders up-to-date regularly has several advantages:

> ▷ **No big surprises**: Incremental updates are rather small than big and can be corrected easier. Big surprises and throwbacks can be avoided.

> ▷ **Short feedback loops**: Aligning with stakeholders opens the feedback loop and gives valuable information not only to

them, but also back. They will tell you, if the like it or not. Find out the reasons and use them to further improve your work.

▷ **Early identification of blockers**: If you have missed something, you will recognize it earlier. This gives you the change to work on the bigger problems earlier.

Example – Blog

One example I perceived positive was the company internal blog of an architecture colleague. He posted from time to time thoughts and results of his work. This way everyone who was interested could receive the latest updated, thoughts, advances and challenges. Feedback or discussions could be started directly underneath the post.

9.5. Be transparent

Regular communication is important, but it mitigates missing transparency only partially. A major outcome of architecture work is options and decisions. To be as transparent as possible, you need to make sure, that all decisions are understandable. Especially, if people are not involved in the decision-making process it is hard to understand and to follow the decision and rationale behind it.

Therefore, it is important to carefully document considered options, their pros and cons and especially, the reason why one option was selected. In Section 5.3 an example of an evaluation process was given.

Benefit

Options have advantages and disadvantages. You will always find someone who will be unhappy with the taken decision. Therefore, it is important to be able to explain, why a certain decision was taken, and that the downsides have been considered. This often calms down people and they realize, that the decision was not taken easily.

In an agile development model, requirements are changing faster than in a waterfall world. This also implies, that taken decisions are more often revisited and even adapted based on new insights. Hence, you need to have a leaner approach to manage decisions.

Example – Decision & Guideline Wiki

All decisions and guidelines should be made transparent to everyone. As some decisions or guidelines may change from time to time, it is a good idea to put them into a wiki. Many people can work and interact with the content easily. Corrections can be made transparent and changes can be communicated automatically, by subscribing to specific topics of interest.

One exemplary structure of how a guideline could look like can be found in Table 9.2. This is an adapted template I used in my doctoral thesis [61]. Within a wiki you can use hyperlinks for referencing guidelines, tree structures to group guidelines by category and many more things to manage guidelines properly. Especially, examples were perceived as helpful and were added and enhanced most often.

9.6. Be always prepared to give a presentation

There is always someone with questions and you want to give the right answers immediately. Try to always have the most important slides in a consolidated form which you can show and explain.

Category and Goals	
Business Goal	Addressed business goal, e.g., time-to-market, reduced IT costs, agility, etc.
Design Principle	Addressed design principle or quality attribute, e.g., standardization, usability
Category	Category of Guideline, e.g., naming convention, data exchange pattern, etc.
Title	Short and crisp summary
Guideline	
Instruction	Description how design principle should be implemented
Criticality	Importance, e.g., nice-to-have, business critical
Reason	Why should this guideline be followed? Includes motivation and background
Alternative	Which alternative options have been discussed and discarded? Why?
Related Guideline	Reference to related guideline (parent or sibling)
Examples	
Positive	Example how guideline can be fulfilled
Negative	Example which violates guideline

Table 9.2.: Template for guidelines

Some ideas to get you started:

▷ **High level architecture diagram**: What are the building blocks of your product or project. What is the purpose of the used components and how are they interlinked with each other.

▷ **High level design principles**: Which architecture style is followed, and which patterns are applied. Ideally, this is motivated by functional and non-functional requirements and business goals, e.g., reduced time-to-market, simplification, etc.

▷ **Latest decisions and prioritized backlog**: What have been done recently and what are the next topics which will be discussed. What are the challenges and how are they tackled.

▷ **Risk and issues**: Which risks, and issues have been identified, who is tackling them, until when are they planned to be resolved.

▷ **Requirements**: What are the most prominent and important functional and non-functional requirements.

▷ **Vision & Roadmap**: What do you want to achieve with the product or project. And what are the bigger milestones or rough plans for the upcoming releases or next years. More on Vision & Roadmap in Sections 12.1 and 12.2.

▷ **Organization chart**: Who is involved in the product development or project. Who are the stakeholders.

Benefit

First, being prepared gives security to yourself. This is like writing cheat sheets for exams. Even if you do not need them, they help. You think about the topics regularly, give them a proper structure and often, you discover topics to improve.

But of course, you will get questions by many people, over and over. At the latest, when things are not working as expected. For example, an increase in bugs, delay in Feature delivery, not met timelines, poor performance of the systems, etc. Then you will be thankful, to have explanations. And, as your information is well structured, hopefully it already includes answers and pain relievers in your backlog or risk and issue list, which only need prioritization.

Example – Structuring open topics

Open topics are everywhere. Unfortunately, they pop up here and there. Giving them a proper structure helps to identify duplicates or similar items and to come up with more. Divide and conquer is a very helpful technique in this context. As described in Section 6.3 you could for example establish layers for your product / application and distribute topics among them. You probably will identify more missing topics while executing this exercise.

The second step is then to give items a priority. You can use for example the WSJF method described in Section 5.2. Some layers need to be tackled earlier and some later, which gives you another helpful indicator for prioritization.

9.7. Avoid slang, irony or sarcasm

Using slang, irony or sarcasm, is a common practice for many people. But in a business context, you should be crisp and clear about what you want to say. You want to make sure, that what you say is also understood. Giving mixed messages by saying one thing and meaning another is not helping. Although, you may think it is fun to do so.

You can have fun before or later, but important statements should be free of potential misunderstandings. Especially, if you are in a multicultural setting, this is important. People with different background are even less likely to interpret mixed messages correctly.

Benefit

By avoiding slang, irony, sarcasm, etc., you can avoid a lot of misunderstandings. If people do not know each other well, the probability is high, that mixed messages are misinterpreted. It unnecessarily leads to misunderstandings and complicated conversations.

Forcing people to read between the lines is dangerous. Interpretations may be wrong or lead to rumors. This undermines your position or sabotages your goals. Further, it can hurt people if you use harsh language too often or offensively, e.g., f*ck.

Example – Irony / Sarcasm

If pronounced correctly and in a specific context, the sentence, "We should not do it, as we always do...", could also mean "There is no doubt about it, that we should do it. Why are we even talking about it?". If you want to say the later, then say it in the first place. Be clear and direct.

10. Estimate and Evaluate

"The key to good decision making is evaluating the available information - the data - and combining it with your own estimates of pluses and minuses. As an economist, I do this every day."

(Emily Oster)

As architect or lead developer you are often asked for estimates to realize your ideas: How long, how much, how many people, which skills, etc. Of course, if you plan to introduce new tools or frameworks you need to have an answer for this kind of questions. Evaluation of new ideas is also required in this context, not only to come up with estimates, but also to understand if you are on the right path.

In this section you will learn the basics of estimation in classical and agile environments. Further, I present some ideas on how to prepare yourself to evaluate "unknown" architectures, which is also often asked for.

Contents

10.1. **Know basics of estimation**

Estimation depends on the applied software development process. In a waterfall world, you estimate differently than in an agile world. Nevertheless, both worlds need estimations to plan work, forecast the achievement or milestones, to ease alignment with external dependencies or to simply prioritize the work order.

A motivational example, why it is so important to learn and use the right tools for estimation, can be found in Figure 10.1. Which line is longer? Before you continue reading, have a look at the picture.

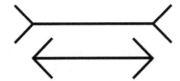

Figure 10.1.: Müller-Leyer Illusion

The answer is: Both lines are of the same length, unless many people believe, that the upper line is longer. This illusion is called Müller-Leyer Illusion [112]. And with that bad sins you are estimating highly complex work? Obviously, proper tools are required for that exercise.

In waterfall projects the scope is fixed, and you want to estimate how long it takes to implement the scope. Hence, an upfront estimation is required which produces an absolute number. Estimating absolute numbers is very difficult. Some approaches have been proposed, two of them are:

> ▷ **Expert estimations:** Experts discuss the planned scope and try, based on their experience from similar projects in the past, to come up with a number. This number is then often adjusted by project managers, to reflect uncertainty, change requests, monetary aspects, testing, etc.

▷ **Estimation frameworks:** COCOMO [94] or the function point analysis [100] are two frameworks which try to give more structure to the estimation process. Both approaches use data from the past and input from the estimated scope to come up with a more realistic estimation which is more a data driven approach and less depended on gut feelings.

Within an agile development setting, the situation looks differently. Of course, you still want to be predictable in what you deliver. But not 2 years, but maybe 10 weeks. The short cycles, i.e. iterations[1], enable to also use past data and experience, to come up with better estimations. Estimation is done mainly with the following tools:

▷ **Relative estimation:** Work items, e.g., User Stories or Features, are estimated with story points, relatively to each other. This is important and a main difference to waterfall estimation. The underlying assumption is, that absolute estimation is not working, but comparing is easier. For example, can you say how tall the Eiffel Tower is? It is easier to say, that it is approx. 80 times higher than a 1 story building.[2]

▷ **Planning poker:** The team sits together and gives relative estimations of the highest prioritized work items to plan them for the next iteration(s). The more often this exercise is done, the better the estimation gets. It further fosters communication to reveal hidden assumptions and clarification of requirements. Based on experience, teams know how many story points can be delivered within a specific period of time. The longer you try to forecast the future, the less accurate the prediction will be, as circumstances may change faster than expected.

---

[1] also called sprint if you use scrum
[2] Nice to know: The height of the Eiffel Tower is 324m

Benefit

Sponsors are always interested in the progress of their products and projects. They want to know when things are ready. With proper estimations, you are able to answer these questions (more or less accurate). And with more data the forecasts are getting better over time.

In an agile world, it seems to be easier to forecast, as work is sliced into smaller pieces and is delivered in form of working software. But as priorities can changed easier, a proper estimation has also pitfalls. Estimations are still a good tool to plan work using story points or to estimate the priorities with WSJF as described in Section 5.2.

On the other hand, in a waterfall project, big chunks of work need big up-front design and estimations. The bigger the work packages are, the less likely it is to get the right estimates. And if changes are introduced late in the process, the change impact is way higher. This needs to be reflected in the estimations as well.

Note: Estimation is a difficult topic, as it contains a uncertainty. There are even people who reject estimating at all. This is then called #NoEstimates.

Example – Naive forecasting in scrum

Assume you have a scrum team working now for 5 iterations. Further, you have a product roadmap containing some Features. Your stakeholders are interested in knowing when these Features are implemented, so that they can start to market them. The team had a rough look at the Features and derived 42 stories. Of course, this is already an estimation, as the stories are not properly groomed, and it may be, that there are stories required to get the Features done. But that's all you have for now.

To make a forecast for the 42 stories, the historic data should be used, given in Table 10.1. The scrum team had 5 iterations and finished

Iteration	1	2	3	4	5
# Stories	4	6	11	8	5
Days	10	10	10	10	8
# Stories/ Day (SD)	0.4	0.6	1.1	0.8	0.625

Table 10.1.: Exemplary historic data of a scrum team

each with different number of stories. The fifth iteration contained two public holidays which could also be considered, to give a more accurate estimation.

The naive approach would be to take the average number of delivered stories per day of the last 5 iterations and extrapolate it to make a forecast. In this case this would mean for the mean m of delivered stories per day:

$$m = \frac{0.4 + 0.6 + 1.1 + 0.8 + 0.625}{5} = 0.705$$

To forecast how many days the 42 stories need, 42 needs to be divided by the mean m of delivered stories per day:

$$\frac{42}{0.705} = 59.57 \approx 60$$

That means, for 42 stories, the scrum team needs 60 days or 6 iterations assuming 10 days per iteration.

Example – Monte Carlo forecasting in scrum

The naive forecasting approach does not take into account the deviation of different iterations. Thus you do not know how likely it is, that the team will finish after 6 iterations. A popular approach to calculate the likelihood for the estimation is to use the Monte Carlo

Method [82, 111]. With the Monte Carlo Method possible outcomes are simulated many times and the results are afterwards aggregated. For example, if you want to estimate the likelihood of rolling a 6 with a dice, you could roll it 1000 times and count how often every number was rolled and divide by the number of rolled sixes to get the likelihood. This is an approximation, but as there is the law of large numbers, the theoretical number will be very close to the simulated one, the more runs the simulation executes [104].

In this example the implementation of the 42 stories is simulated 1000 times. There are only 5 historic values for SD available which is not enough for a proper simulation. Therefore, an initial sampling to bootstrap the simulation is necessary: Out of the 5 historic SD values, 5 series of 1000 random picks are generated S_1 to S_5. Samples are now calculated by calculating an average: $(S_1[i] + S_2[i] + S_3[i] + S_4[i] + S_5[i])/5$. This generates a list of 1000 new values all between 0.4 and 1.1. Let's call this value SDB and the list SDB[].

For every value SDB out of SDB[], do the following: Divide the number of stories, which should be estimated, by SDB, which gives the number of days for completing the stories. The result divided by the number of days per sprint gives the number of iterations required.

$$\frac{\#\text{stories}}{\text{SDB}} = \text{days} \qquad \frac{\text{days}}{\#\text{days/iteration}} = \#\text{iterations}$$

Finally, round up the result of #iterations. Now the 1000 results can be aggregated in a histogram properly.

The derivation of 1000 simulations, assuming 42 stories to be completed and 10 days per iteration, results in the diagram depicted in Figure 10.2. Because of the random factor, it will look differently if the simulation is repeated. The height of the bars indicates, how often a specific bucket (number of iterations) was simulated. 6 iterations were the outcome of most simulations as calculated with the

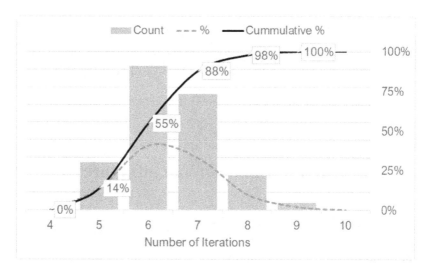

Figure 10.2.: Statistics of 1000 simulations regarding number of required iterations

naive average method. The dotted line is the distribution, and the solid line the cumulative distribution of iterations.

With a likelihood of 55%, the 42 stories will be done after 6 iterations. In statistics, a likelihood of 95% is usually high enough, hence, 8 iterations would be the best estimation to finish the 42 stories. To be 100% certain, you need to plan 9 iterations.

You can find the spread sheet to dig deeper and repeat the experiment here:

 Simple forecasting in Scrum with Monte Carlo Simulation (http://bit.ly/2u1JWmL)

Further Reading

▷ **Agile Estimating and Planning** [18] by Mike Cohn

▷ **Cost estimation with COCOMO II** [12] by Barry W. Boehm

10.2. Evaluate "unknown" architecture

Architecture reviews or supporting teams to cope with challenges of their current architecture is a common exercise. Good architects are rare and of high demand. Hence, supporting "unknown" projects or products will happen. And you want to do a good job.

You can prepare yourself for it, by having a set of questions at hand which are common. And it's not only about architecture, but also about how the development process works or how the application is operated. Some ideas for general questions:

▷ **Design practices**: Which principles and patterns does the architecture follow? Are they consequently and correctly used? Does the design follow a red line or is there an uncontrolled growth? Is there a clear structure and separation of concerns?

▷ **Development practices**: Code guidelines in place and followed? How is the code versioned? Deployment practices?

▷ **Quality assurance**: Test automation? Code coverage? Static code analysis in place and good results? Peer reviews in place?

▷ **Security**: Which security concepts are in place? Built-in security? Penetration tests or automated security analysis tools in place and regularly used?

Benefit

Asking the right questions helps to identify the good and the bad things of an application architecture easier. Looking on (architecture) diagrams alone is usually not helping. They are often outdated or lack of proper explanations.

For me, architecture is involved everywhere in software development. Architecture must be considered in requirements engineering, development, testing, releasing, operations, etc. Hence, all aspects need to be checked during a review, to identify all potential gaps.

Evaluating unknown architectures, is helping to broaden your knowledge and opening your horizon. You will see different challenges and plenty of solutions. All with their pros and cons. Learning and incorporating this knowledge will make you a better architect.

Example – Decoupling of Deployment and Release

Nowadays, it's a popular practice to deploy often and continuously into production, without releasing any new Feature. Features are released "on-demand". This is often done with Feature toggles, which means, that Features are deployed, but hidden for the mass behind a configuration "flag" and can be toggled on and off.

To help teams adopting this practice, you need to understand not only their architecture, but also the whole development process, from idea to cash:

▷ **Requirement**: How are requirements sliced? Can they be independently developed from the rest of the code or are they causing side effects if one Feature is not in place for another?

▷ **Development**: Can feature toggles or similar techniques be integrated into the code?

▷ **Testing**: Are regression tests in place? How high is the code coverage?

▷ **Automation:** Is build, test and deployment automated?

▷ **Monitoring**: How do you detect anomalies or errors?

▷ **Recovery**: If something goes wrong, can you go back or fix forward?

This is just an excerpt of questions which I would ask in this context. They are based on typical development practices as well as to the concrete challenge. It would be possible to simply get the Feature toggles implemented, but what happens, if you activate a Feature and it causes site effects? You may not have tested it well enough, you may not identify problems because of missing monitoring, you may not be able to recover, etc.

I believe, that architects need to look at the full picture. Implementing the new cool pattern, because it was advertised somewhere, without looking left and right, will lead to severe issues.

11. Balance

> *"In contradiction and paradox, you can find truth."*

(Denis Villeneuve)

The more non-functional requirements are requested, the lower the throughput of functional requirements will be. If you request a 100% test coverage, it will obviously take longer to implement a Feature: Writing so many tests will take time. Demanding a fully configurable product, will take significantly more time than delivering a "fixed" product. And the complexity will raise. As architect it is your job to negotiate between different stakeholders and their demands. And you are also a stakeholder which makes it even more difficult to negotiate.

In this section you will learn the impact of demanding high quality, the impact of contradicting goals and how to handle them with some basics of conflict management. Finding the right balance between functional and non-functional requirements, will help you to achieve goals with a reasonable quality.

Contents

117

11.1. Quality comes at a price

Earlier I wrote about quality and non-functional requirements. The more quality and non-functional requirements a system needs to fulfill, the more effort this will require. The DevOps principle decoupling of deployment and release, described in Section 10.2, is one example of a non-functional requirement which causes high effort to realize. Many practices need to be in place, before the principle can be applied.

In general, the more quality constraints and non-functional requirement need to be fulfilled, the more effort, budget and time this will cost. You need to find the right balance between functional and non-functional requirements. Over-engineering must be avoided.

You should lay out the impact of specific non-functional requirements early in the project. Everyone should understand the consequences of specific requirements. Specific non-functional requirements also have an impact on functional requirements which may not be desired. It is an architect's job to consult and educate on those topics.

Benefit

Working out and knowing early the consequences of non-functional requirements is beneficial in two aspects:

▷ **Expectation management**: Everyone can be brought on the same page regarding consequences on budget, effort and time. It is easier to act in an environment where consequences are transparent and clarified.

▷ **Architectural runway**: If agreed, the required steps, to fulfill the non-functional requirements, can be derived and planned accordingly.

For agile projects, the Definition of Done (DoD) can be adapted, to reflect the quality attributes. If expectation management was done properly, no one should be surprised, that the development speed will decrease, the more quality and non-functional requirements need to be considered.

Example – Uber Testing

If you want to make sure, that your code is working correctly in every circumstance, you can try to force developers to write gazillions of test cases, all automated, and covering all possible execution paths within the code including all possible value combinations. Alternatively, you can insist on mathematically proofing the correctness of the code. If you want to fly to the moon, then this may be the right approach, as you cannot try out the code easily, and correct it without losing a rocket and some million dollars every time.

In general, this kind of Uber Testing is a bad idea. It will slow down development significantly. But finding the right balance is also not easy. Is it 100% test coverage or 95%? This is just a value, but it does not tell, if the right tests have been written. Aiming at specific percentages is also difficult, as some developers start to game the system by writing empty or dummy tests, just to fulfill the numbers.

My advice is to continuously conduct workshops and training sessions regarding test practices. Developers need to exchange their ideas and experience of good and bad test practices and figure out the right balance to fulfill the demanded quality and non-functional requirements.

Further Reading

▷ **Test-driven development: by example** [9] by Kent Beck

119

11.2. Solve contradicting goals

Different groups and people within an organization have usually different goals and directions. This is especially true for different departments or product and project organizations within an organization.

A classic example of contradicting goals is short- and long-term goals. Projects often tend to build the simplest solution, whereas an organization has a long-term vision in mind. Often, the simple solution does not fit into the long-term solution and is at risk to be thrown away later. To avoid implementation into the wrong direction, two things should be considered:

▷ Developers and business need to understand the long-term vision and their benefits to adapt their solution and

▷ managers who are responsible for budget need to be involved to understand the financial impact.

It is not necessary to have 100% of the long-term vision implemented directly. But the developed piece of software should be laid out to add or support the long-term vision.

Note: This topic is very tough. From a software architecture position, it can often not be solved. But you can make the problems and challenges transparent and support their solution on different layers.

Benefit

Having contradicting goals cancels out the invested effort as illustrated in Figure 11.1 (compare with Moore [57]). Each vector has a direction, which is the strategy or goal and a magnitude which represents the effort. If people and teams are not aligned and in sync, their effort simply cancels out. This is the visualization of the feeling,

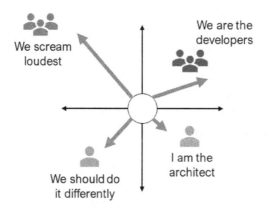

Figure 11.1.: Missing alignment cancels out effort.

that everyone in the company is busy and working hard, but no or only little progress is made.

By aligning the people and teams, and solving the contradicting goals, the effort which is invested will not cancel out anymore and the progress will increase.

Example – Automation

A new CRM system should be implemented. For some reasons, it was decided to not use a standard product from a vendor, but to do a custom implementation. From a project or product development perspective, the goal is clear: The defined (minimum) requirements need to be implemented as fast as possible.

Some architects appear and tell the development team, to foresee APIs, because the CRM system should be integrated into automated business processes. The product owner or project lead will of course try to reject that requirement, as it is not relevant now. And this is totally fine (for now). But, the development team needs to foresee, that this requirement needs to be fulfilled later, and already consider an implementation which does not hinder exposing APIs. Further, they need to fit into the context of the business process which may also have an impact of the functional requirements of the system itself.

Instead of everyone doing what they want, an alignment with the overall vision and strategy is meaningful and could help the whole organization to move into the same direction and achieve more with less.

11.3. Conflict management

Architects are often the glue between multiple groups with different backgrounds. This may lead to conflicts on different levels of communication. To find a balanced solution which also reflect long-term, strategic goals, it is often the role of architects to help overcome the conflict.

My starting point regarding communication theory was the "Four-Sides Model" by Schulze von Thun [99, 86]. Based on this model a lot can be shown and deducted. The four sides model is depicted in Figure 11.2.

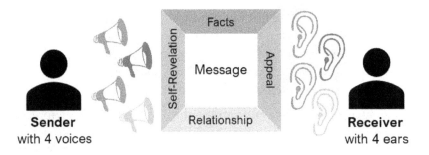

Figure 11.2.: Four-Sides Model by Schulze von Thun [86]

According to the four sides model [86, 99] a message (communication) has four facets, though not the same emphasis might be put on each. The four facets are:

▷ **Factual Information**: Statements that contain data and facts.

▷ **Self-revelation**: Tells something about the sender, its motives, values, emotions etc.

▷ **Relationship**: Contains information about the relationship between sender and receiver, i.e., what the sender thinks about the receiver.

▷ **Appeal**: Contains the desire, advice, instruction and effects that the speaker is seeking.

A message can be sent, as well as received, with emphasis on one of the four sides. And this mismatch can lead to misunderstandings. To avoid this, you can apply two techniques.

▷ **Think before you communicate:** As a sender, think about your intention and what you want the other to do. As a receiver, think about which ear you currently use, what information the sender might want to send and how else the message could be understood.

▷ **Validate the message**: As a sender, make the intention of your message clear and explicit. Ask what the receiver has heard. As a receiver, ask questions back, to check if you understood properly what was said.

Note: I think, applying conflict management techniques is key to communication. Be open-minded and try (honestly) to understand your communication partner. Be aware of the facts mentioned above. And do not worry, if it does not work out well. Communication is difficult. And sometimes people are just not willing to listen and block communication.

Benefit

By understanding and accepting the fact, that communication is difficult, you can act on it. You will have situations in which you want to negotiate or try to solve contradicting goals or different design options. Then, you need to have the right communication techniques to handle the situations. With the two laid-out checking techniques, you can reduce misunderstandings.

My advice is to go to a communication seminar and learn it hands on. It is very difficult to learn it from books. They can make you aware of some the effects and causes, but they probably cannot help to fix or improve communication as required in today's demanding world.

Example

Assume, you want to talk with a developer about a specific architecture aspect of a solution. You approach the developer and say: "I would like to talk with you about the design, I have some remarks.". As a sender you wanted to say the following:

> ▷ **Factual**: "I want to talk about the design."
>
> ▷ **Self-revealing**: "I have a question and would like to clarify it."
>
> ▷ **Relationship**: "I would like to share my ideas with you."
>
> ▷ **Appeal**: "Let's talk."

But the developer, may receive the following message:

> ▷ **Factual**: "You want to talk about the design."
>
> ▷ **Self-revealing**: "You think my design makes no sense."
>
> ▷ **Relationship**: "You think I am stupid."
>
> ▷ **Appeal**: "I need to change my design."

Communication can lead very easily to misunderstandings. Hence, invest more time to explain yourself, what you want and why. Do not assume, that your counterpart directly understands the same.

Further Reading

▷ **Miteinander reden: Störungen und Klärungen** (german) [86] by Friedemann Schulz von Thun

▷ English alternative: Four-sides model on wikipedia [99]

12. Consult and Coach

"I wasn't naturally gifted in terms of size and speed; everything I did in hockey I worked for, and that's the way I'll be as a coach."

(Wayne Gretzky)

Being pro-active is probably the best you can do when it comes to consulting and coaching. If you are asked, it is often too late. And cleaning up fundamental failure within software architecture is something, which you want to avoid. You need to somehow foresee future and prepare yourself and the organization for the next steps. This is not simple, but some techniques exist to catch current discussions and lead into a specific direction.

In this section you will learn more about visions, roadmaps and maturity models, and how to use them to give purpose and guidance. Further, I give you tips on leading by questions, align people using community of practices and why to be or become trustworthy.

Contents

12.1. Have a vision

You always need to have a vision of your long-term goals. This is usually used by business people to describe and define their business, product or corporate identity. I believe, that it is important to also have a complementary technical vision which supports the business vision.

As architect you should have a *vision statement* for the system, the product or the entire organization: A story of who, why, what, when, where, and how. A vision statement is a tool for telling a part of this story, helping to create a picture in everyone's head, which is the north-star, where you want to strive towards.

Popular vision statements are brief, memorable, unique, realistic and current [67]. But this is not easy to achieve. A helpful tool to get you started creating a compelling vision statement is the following template, which is based on Moore's [59] template for product visions:

> ▷ **For** "target group"

> ▷ **Who** "needs or has pains with"

> ▷ **The** "product name"

> ▷ **Is a** "new product category"

> ▷ **That** "product benefit, reason to adopt"

> ▷ **Unlike** "competitors, alternatives"

> ▷ **Our product** "differentiation, features, value proposition"

From an architect's point of view, you may replace "product" with a specific technology, framework, methodology or infrastructure component which you want to advertise. But, of course, you can also describe it from a product perspective, if there is no business vision in place. I think, describing it from a product perspective has the strongest impact on motivation and alignment. And as more and

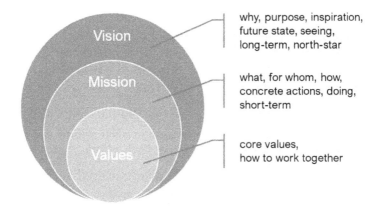

Figure 12.1.: Vision, Mission and Values

more products are tech products anyway, the difference between technical and business vision is getting smaller.

Based on the vision statement, a concrete mission statement and values can be derived. The vision statement is the future state, whereas the mission statement describes what needs to be done now, and some details on the how. Of course, the mission should comply to the vision. And the values often describe how you want to work together. Compare Figure 12.1. Unlike other authors, I believe, that the vision statement should already contain the why. The why is very powerful to give a purpose.

Benefit

Having a proper vision eases the understanding why you are working for a company or on a specific product. It aligns people to work on a common goal. The motivational aspect is key. Why are you doing all these things? People need a purpose. They desire to do something that has meaning and is important. [69]

A vision can inspire people which opens new energy to work against and give their best. US president John F. Kennedy for example inspired the nation to fly to the moon in his speech "We choose to go to the Moon" [125]. This vision inspired "the nation" and the space mission of the NASA was derived out of it.

If your vision contains for example the simplification of your products or systems, then this ease or even enables people to accept and propose trade-offs which was not possible before.

Finally, a vision is usefully as an elevator pitch. What are you doing? Why is it important? Then you have a great and simple answer.

Example – Apples Vision Statement

"We believe that we are on the face of the earth to make great products and that's not changing. We are constantly focusing on innovating. We believe in the simple not the complex. We believe that we need to own and control the primary technologies behind the products that we make and participate only in markets where we can make a significant contribution. We believe in saying no to thousands of projects, so that we can really focus on the few that are truly important and meaningful to us. We believe in deep collaboration and cross-pollination of our groups, which allow us to innovate in a way that others cannot. And frankly, we don't settle for anything less than excellence in every group in the company, and we have the self-honesty to admit when we're wrong and the courage to change. And I think regardless of who is in what job those values are so embedded in this company that Apple will do extremely well." [47]

The first statement is already very powerful. It defines the purpose: "make great products". One strong statement in this vision is to focus on projects which matter. This enables people to say no, and to reject or abort experiments which are not leading anywhere, without the fear to blame anyone.

This vision statement also contains values, like self-honesty or courage. With that, it defines how people should interact with each other. Having core values is important. But even more important is, that they are lived. Hence, whatever you write down into your vision statement, make sure that you act accordingly. If you tell people to build cross-functional teams, then enable it by tearing down the silos.

Further Reading

▷ **Drive: The Surprising Truth About What Motivates Us** [69] by Daniel H. Pink

▷ **Crossing the Chasm: Marketing and Selling Disruptive Products to Mainstream Customers** [59] by Geoffrey A. Moore

 Start with why (YouTube) **by Simon Sinek** (http://bit.ly/2J0wd9j)

12.2. Use roadmaps and maturity models

You cannot achieve everything at once, it is a journey. Therefore, I prefer to use roadmaps or maturity models. They give a structure which can be easily consumed and reflect the status and progress towards the goals. Unlike a vision statement, they include more concrete items towards one can work.

For different aspects I use different roadmaps or maturity models, e.g., development practices or continuous delivery. All models have in common, that they have a fixed amount of levels. I usually use 4 to 5 levels. Every maturity level is clearly defined. And only if all criteria are fulfilled, the level is reached. This makes sense, as implementing an item from a higher level is likely not giving you the full benefit if the lower levels are not fully implemented yet. They are sometimes even prerequisites.

Setting up a maturity model can be done bottom-up or top-down. Using the top-down approach, you first define the number of levels and put into the level the specific characteristics, which you think should be fulfilled. With the bottom-up approach, you first identify the characteristics you want to have and afterwards cluster them. This may result then in a x-level model or something different.

Regardless of how you come up with the maturity model, it is important, that everyone understands the criteria which are required to reach the next level. I suggest using the common practice of SMART criteria [23, 119]: Specific, measurable, achievable, realistic, time-bounded. Time-bounded is not that important for a maturity model. But giving indications of the time horizon is important. Are you talking about months, years or even decades?

Benefit

Maturity models give structure. You can derive a plan to achieve the next level in the model. If all criteria are fulfilled, the next level is achieved. Hence, it is very important to have the criteria defined properly, otherwise you end up in discussing over and over the fulfillment of the criteria. The level structure gives a clear prioritization, of which action needs to be taken next.

Studies show, that if maturity models are interlinked with business benefits, this can lead to improved confidence of business sponsors that their investments will return business benefits [32]. Initiatives can be evaluated against their added value regarding the maturity model and investments can be planned more wisely.

If standardized maturity models are used, e.g., CMMI [93, 92] or SPICE [17, 102], it is even possible to compare your company's maturity with competitors. And, if desired, act on it and improve.

Example – Visualization Methods

Developing and describing a detailed maturity model is out of scope of this book. Some more concrete maturity models can be found in the "further reading" section. Still, some examples on how to visualize maturity models is helpful.

Figure 12.2 includes four different visualization techniques for maturity models:

> ▷ **Matrix**: Ideal for many information and details. Usually, many bullet points are included in the boxes and it is hard to read in a presentation. But ideal, for handouts and actual work.

> ▷ **Spider Web**: Ideal for comparing different topics, companies or progress, e.g., last and current year, with each other. Easy to identify the weak spots.

> ▷ **Stairway to Heaven** or **Pyramid**: High level overview with focus on "higher is better". Detail description for every step can be included as well.

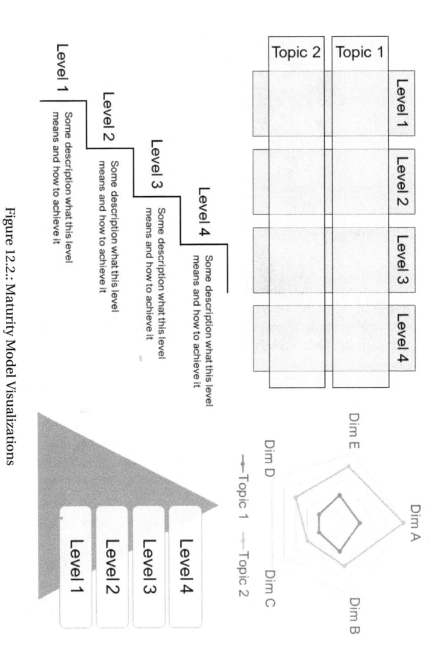

Figure 12.2.: Maturity Model Visualizations

Further Reading

Exemplary Continues Delivery Maturity Model
[3] (http://bit.ly/2H4EvLd)

Digital Transformation: A Stairway to Heaven
[58] by Geoffrey Moore (http://bit.ly/2ZUMFx3)

12.3. Build a community of practice (CoP)

Exchanging experience and knowledge among a common group of interest helps distributing ideas and standardizing approaches. For example, you could gather all JavaScript developers and architects in one room, continuously, e.g., every month, and discuss past and current challenges and how they were tackled, or new methodologies and approaches which they are applying.

According to Wenger [88] "Communities of practice are groups of people who share a concern or a passion for something they do and learn how to do it better as they interact regularly". CoPs can be established independently from the development approach. Practitioners from line-organizations, waterfall projects as well as from agile projects can participate in such groups. According to Wenger [88] people need to have a combination of the following three elements, which Figure 12.3 summarizes:

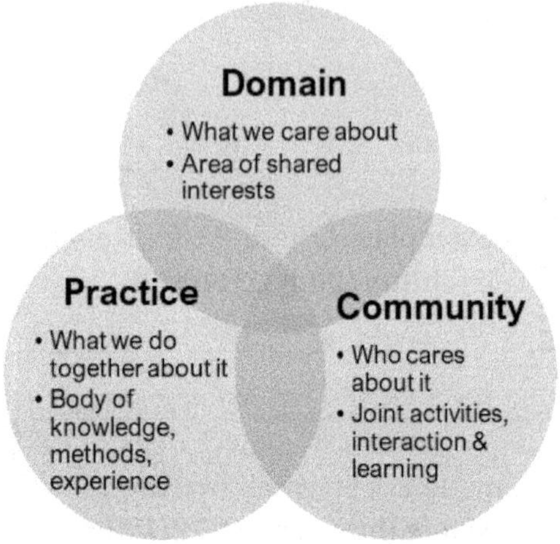

Figure 12.3.: Community of Practice

▷ **Domain**: People have an area of shared interests. It's not a club of friends. People within the same domain have a shared competency and therefore distinguish themselves from other people.

▷ **Community**: Members have joint activities and discussions within their domain. They interact, learn, help and share information with each other. People, who have the same job title or interest are not forming a community, unless they interact and learn together. However, it's not essential to work together daily to be a community.

▷ **Practice**: People within a community of practice need to be *practitioners* within their domain. That requires knowledge, methods, experience, skills, stories, patterns, ways of addressing challenges, etc. It is not a community of interests.

Common activities of CoPs are: problem solving, discussing developments, executing visits or gemba[1] walks, share or seek experience, requesting information, document, and many more.

CoPs should be formed by practitioners who are willing to change something. It makes no sense to dictate forming this group and forcing them to participate in the activities. Practitioners within this group must have a motivation for collaboration by themselves. Sometimes, it is already enough to have one or two motivated people who initiate a CoP and act as a catalyst. Others may get motivated to join.

You may know CoPs under a different term. They are also called for example learning networks, user groups or tech clubs. And they come in various forms. In agile frameworks they are even explicitly mentioned, to align people across different teams. Within SAFe, this is also called community of practice. Within the spotify model it's called guild. But however, you call it, the purpose is very similar in all cases.

Benefit

Architects can share, discuss and align their visions, developers can share challenges, solutions and experience. An exchange of knowledge, skills and experience across the organization can take place. This network gives access to expertise to help solving challenges but also to enable (continuous) learning and improvement from each other.

For an organization, CoPs are highly beneficial in terms of rapid problem-solving, improved quality or increased cooperation across the whole organization, within one or multiple domains. But it's also beneficial for the individual to create a stronger network of experts, who can support solving difficult challenges with their ideas and knowledge.

---

[1]Where the work is done

Example – Align on technology

An architecture CoP at Zalando has created the Technology Radar, highlighted in Figure 7.2. People from different teams come together and discuss the current challenges and possible solutions. They align on technology they want to use or which they want to try out. And they also clearly say, what they do not want to use (anymore).

Such an alignment is especially important in a microservice-oriented architecture, where often per default, every technology can be used. From an enterprise perspective it makes sense to agree on some standards, e.g., an infrastructure standard, such as AWS. This can reduce costs, eases maintenance, knowledge about technology is spread, instead of having highly specialized people within every team, etc.

Further Reading

▷ **Communities of practice: Learning, meaning, and identity** [88] by Etienne Wenger

▷ **How to Do a Gemba Walk: Coaching Gemba Walkers** [14] by Michael Bremer

Community of Practice on the SAFe Website [41] (http://bit.ly/2JkafgL)

12.4. Conduct open-door sessions

One source of misconceptions or ambiguity is lack of communication. One solution is to block a fixed time slot, e.g., 30-60 min every week, for talking about hot topics with developers, your architect peers or other stakeholders. This session is for you, if you have the feeling that you or others are not well enough aligned and cannot participate in all meetings of the team(s) as you take care of many.

This session has no agenda everything can be discussed. Everyone collects topics. Try to solve minor challenges or questions on the spot. Schedule follow-ups on the more complex topics.

Benefit

The major benefit of having an open-door session is to make you approachable. Often architects are busy, and it is difficult to catch them. Scheduling individual meetings is cumbersome. Having a fixed time slot eases this situation.

It gives a different option to exchange and discuss topics, versus strict decision-making sessions. Alignment is important, and these sessions foster alignment.

Further, and probably most important, an open door is very welcoming. From my perspective it is important to create a safe environment, where everything may be asked and discussed. For other people it may not be clear why specific decisions were made or goals were defined and how they reflect in day to day work. For developers as well as for peer architects and managers.

Benefit for you, as an architect, is to gain better insights. What are the concrete challenges developers are currently facing? Maybe, some of them are not visible to you if you are detached. What do other architects think of your decisions? Maybe they have some tips to improve your work. What do business sponsors think of the project or product implementation? Are the business goals still valid? This may influence your decision-making process.

Example

No example. Just do it.

12.5. Lead by asking questions

Guiding people with concrete answers, decisions or solutions is great
and needs to be done as part of the consultant mindset. But there is
one more powerful way: Leading people with questions to answers
or solutions. I prefer to use this technique if I want to educate others,
in becoming better at thinking and solving problems by themselves,
or if I have a group of people who is likely to not accept my saying,
e.g., they think I'm dump, or they are just suspicious in general about
the direction of architecture guidance.

You can lead people into a specific direction of thinking by asking the
right questions. This way, they will find out how to solve a problem by
themselves. You do not need to present them the answer and explain
the pros and cons and conduct a discussion why this is correct. Instead, they come up with the answer by themselves and already like
the solution which *you* can challenge and let them defend it. This
even strengthens their preference for the solution.

That an interviewer can influence the answers of an interviewee has
been demonstrated in several psychological experiments, e.g., [50].
Some techniques which you can use to lead or even persuade people
into a specific direction are the following:

> ▷ **Closed-ended question**: You limit the choice of the answers
> by asking: "Do you prefer A or B?". Whereas A *and* B are your
> preferred solutions, or one solution is good and the other is so
> bad, that it cannot be chosen. You omit other options and limit
> the solution space.

▷ **Framed question**: Using specific phrases like "Do you agree to ..." can lead into a specific direction. If people have the tendency to say 'yes', you use it to get your ideas through. If they tend to say 'no', use it to exclude some alternatives which you dislike.

▷ **Foot-in-the-door technique**: Start asking for small things which are easy to agree for the person. Later in the discussion, or better some days later, ask for larger things. The likelihood increases to get positive answers to the larger request. Experiments demonstrate, that "once someone has agreed to a small request he is more likely to comply with a larger request.". [29]

Note: In a healthy environment there shouldn't be a need to influence people. They are already part of the architecture process and hence, aligned. Unfortunately, in many environments this is not the case. If your task is to enforce specific architecture decisions which have been made without the people who need to implement them, then this technique is the better approach. Alternatives like forcing people or putting them under pressure, is not healthy and not sustainable. The results are often inferior.

Benefit

Based on my observations, people who are told what to do, are less motivated to actually do it. If a group of people is suspicions, has distrust or an aversion against you or the direction of the architecture in general, you can come with the best solution on earth, they will challenge it. Then you will have a hard time to convince them. This is usually something what you want to avoid.

With leading questions, you can turn around the game and let them come up with the solution you desire, but they think that it is their own solution. This way you take yourself out of the line of fire, but you can still lead them into a specific direction. Framing the situation properly is important: You need to make clear, that you are there to help them finding the best way, given the current business goals.

Example – Social Conformity

Another approach to lead into a specific direction is based on the following experiment: Solomon Asch [6] conducted a study in 1955, where he interviewed individuals on their opinion of specific matters. Afterwards they were asked to state their opinion again, but this time they were first told of opinions from authorities or large groups of their peers. Many changed their opinions to the opposing view. Even without arguments, many have accepted a contrary view, just to conform.

A later experiment of him pushed the boundaries even further. A group of people was presented with 3 lines and should compare it to a base line. All people in the group were told to give the wrong answer, except of one. The person who was not told to give the wrong answer, somehow conformed to the answers by the others and gave a wrong answer, too, just to conform.

In a different group setup, the test person got a "partner" giving the right answer. This reduced the conformity of the test person significantly, and he gave the right answers. Without a "partner" but allowed to write down the answers to stay anonymously, the rate of right answers also increased significantly.

Thus, opinions can be influenced not only by leading with the right questions, but also by the group setup. Opinions of authorities and peers matter. And people can be influenced by social pressure significantly.

Asch's conformity experiment (YouTube)
(http://bit.ly/2JdPa8B)

12.6. Be trustworthy

As a consultant or coach, you need to be a trusted partner. If people don't trust you, then it is hard to steer them into a specific direction. Think of a football or soccer coach. If players don't trust the coach, the likelihood is low, that this coach will be successful. If a coach is fired, an often-mentioned reason is, that the coach didn't reach the team anymore. As there is also politics around, this may not be always true in the first place, but is a good indication, how important trust is.

But what is trust. And when do people trust you? I found this nice formula, which tries to explain the ingredients of trustworthiness. According to Maister et. al. [51] the formula looks like this:

$$\text{Trustworthiness} = \frac{\text{Credibility} + \text{Reliability} + \text{Intimacy}}{\text{Self-orientation}}$$

▷ **Credibility**. What you say and which skills and credentials you bring with you is an important building block. If you have the wrong background, it is difficult to build up trust. Further, the way you apply your experience and expertise makes a difference.

▷ **Reliability**. Being predictable and dependable in our actions builds trust. Thus, standing to your words and promises is important. Also, not only talk, but act according to your sayings.

Having too many excuses lowers your reliability. Either, don't promise, or get it done.

▷ **Intimacy**. People feel comfortable with you and can confide secrets or unpleasant stories with you. Your discretion keeps those things safe. Thus, always speak positive about other people. Don't slander. Do not create or fuel rumors. Avoid politics the best you can.

▷ **(Low) self-orientation**. The more people feel, that your primary goal is to make them succeed and supporting them in reaching their goals, the more they will trust you. Ideally, their goals are also your goals. If you have your own agenda, people will recognize it soon, and this will lead to loss of trust.

Benefit

Being trustworthy is not only positive for your personal and your company's success, but it also gives you a positive feeling. People will give you more information and insights. You can build better relationships with other people. Networking is very important.

If you want to push forward specific topics, this is often only possible with the support of your colleagues. But they will only follow and support you, if they can trust you. Of course, you also need to trust them. But as always, architect often needs to take the first step.

You can act as a role model and make the company a better place. I believe, that if everyone is trustworthy, then a lot of problems will disappear. People do not need to protect their teams or departments so heavily anymore. People can work better together.

Example – Build up trust

If people do not trust your saying, then whatever you propose or say, will be challenged. The chances are high, that they will come up with their own counter proposals, just because they think and feel, that you have no clue. With trust, this behavior can be reduced to a normal, open, healthy and productive discussion.

If you are new to a team or company, there is often not much trust in place towards you. You first need to proof yourself. Unless, you are a known expert for a topic, then this is often easier. But it can also happen to those experts. Thus, talking to people, and demonstrating the attributes mentioned above, is very important. You are not their enemy, but someone who wants to help them being or becoming better, without having a hidden agenda. And whatever they say, ask or discuss stays in the room.

I was quite young as I got the role as architect. Already my age was something which made me not trustworthy. People said: "How should this young guy help us? We are developing since decades, and he just started and has no experience." The truth is, that I started my professional career 2 years back in a different department as SAP developer. So, I already knew the company and its specialties. And during university, I already gained 5 years experience in online business as software engineer. So, I was not *that* inexperienced. But I had to proof it.

One secret why I was successful at this company was probably, that I was not only a PowerPoint architect, but implemented and managed the central message broker. When there was a question about (web-) services or data integration, I was the person who was asked and knew the answers. The same was true for my colleague. We both knew nearly everything about the service integration within the company. And when there was an incident in production, we were often the first who were asked to give ideas of possible root causes.

Expertise and experience helped a lot. But also, the willingness of helping and solving problems of others gave me a good reputation. I always tried to adjust my goals towards the company goals. And sometimes, I even decided to have more effort on my side, although

I could have avoided it, as I was in the position to decide. People trusted me for my actions and behavior, and I could grow into an enterprise architect role as well. I could talk to many people company wide, many already knew me and how I worked. This way I was able, to steer difficult discussions. I realized the reasons many years later: They have trusted me.

Further Reading

▷ **The trusted advisor** [51] by Maister et. al.

 You can test your trustworthiness (http://bit.ly/2PMgATC)

First why and then trust (YouTube) by Simon Sinek (http://bit.ly/2JUPp8e)

13. Market

"The best marketing doesn't feel like marketing."

(Tom Fishburne)

Your ideas are great, and you have communicated them well, but still nobody wants to follow? Then you probably lack marketing. My personal view on marketing is, that it feels like a double-edged sword. On the one side, it helps you to spread your ideas and people are more likely to prefer your options and solutions. But on the other side, this comes at a cost. Some strategies are less about facts, but they utilize some manipulative, influencing techniques. Hence, be careful, when using such techniques. But even if you decide yourself to not apply manipulative techniques, it is important to know them. Not everyone around you is playing fair, and sometimes you need to protect yourself against manipulation.

In this section you will learn some marketing (manipulation) techniques which can help you to convince others. Use them wisely.

Contents

13.1. Motivate and convince

How do companies convince you to buy a product? They demonstrate its value and benefits. But not with a boring PowerPoint presentation and 5 bullet points. They wrap it nicely and make it as easy as possible to digest. And you can do this, too. Some simple techniques help:

▷ **Prototypes**: Show a prototype of your idea. There are plenty of tools for creating prototypes. In the context of enterprises, which often use SAP software, check out build.me, in which you can create nice looking and clickable UI5 apps, fast and easy. Afterwards, you can even export the html code and use it to kick-start the development. One of my favorite tools to create (mobile) click prototypes is Marvel[1].

▷ **Show a video**: Instead of using "boring slides" you can also show a video which demonstrates your idea, mission or even vision. Motivational music with some impressive images and a little bit of text can act like a catalyst for your ideas. Often there are already marketing videos available for the concept or product you would like to propose from product or consultant companies. If not, there are plenty of tools, which support you in creating simple but impressive videos in minutes, e.g., Adobe Spark, Biteable or mysimpleshow.

▷ **Choose the right time**: The hour of meeting has an impact on the outcome. Studies show, that if people are hungry or tired, and they need to decide, they tend to take a shortcut to keep it as simple as possible for them [20]. Hence, better avoid times where people are hungry or tired, if you want to get some positive discussions.

▷ **Bring people into the right mood**: Before talking about your

---

[1] https://marvelapp.com

new idea or showing them a prototype or video, it is usually a good idea to bring them into the right mood. Do not directly show them your things, but start with simple things, which they already know and like. Build positive tension and curiosity. At best, this starts already some days before the meeting. Make them hungry to see it, like Apple, Microsoft or Google are doing it, before every event where they unveil their newest things.

Warning: Don't overdo this: In the long term, content is king. If your words do not come true, this will damage your reputation in the long term.

Benefit

Technical people tend to be fact oriented. But being fact oriented only, is not really working if you want or need to sell your ideas and options. To emphasize your facts, it is helpful to bring people into the right mood and engaging their emotions with beautiful design and motivational music.

Oswald et al. [66] found out, that people who are happier, are more productive. Within their experiments they measured an increase of 12%. Hence, showing a short motivational video, to bring people in a state of higher energy, is actually a good idea, to get them not only more motivated, but also to be more productive.

Experiments of Barsade [7] demonstrate, that if positive emotions swap over to other group members, they experience improved co-operation, decreased conflicts, and increased perceived task performance. Hence, if you feel and express positive emotions, by yourself or with some help of videos, others are more likely to respond favorable.

Example

No example. I do not want to advertise advertisements.

13.2. Find allies

Establishing or enforcing ideas or concepts on your own can be hard or even impossible. Try to find allies who can support and help convincing others. Use your network. If you do not have one yet, start building it now. You could start by talking to your (open-minded) peers about your ideas. If they like it, or at least parts of it, it is likely that they support your idea ("The idea by X was interesting."). If they don't like it, ask for the reasons: Maybe you have missed something? Or your story is not convincing enough?

The next step is to find allies with decision power. Ask for an open-minded discussion. If you fear the discussion, remember that sometimes you need to leave your comfort zone.

Finally, you should know your surrounding well. Who is a promoter, who is a detractor? Who is influencing whom, and who has the decision power. The more complex the topic is, the more people need to be influenced. Sometimes it is helpful to use a more structured approach. One popular framework to support this activity is power mapping [115]. "Power mapping is a framework for addressing issues and problem solving through leveraging relationships and networks." [19] With this framework, you can determine and visualize the network of people which need to be influenced, in order to influence the target to act in your favor. The mapping works as follows [19, 115, 34]:

> ▷ **Identify the problem:** What do you want to achieve? Example: "We need to introduce microservices."

▷ **Identify major institutions**: Who are key decision makers? Start with institutions, departments, groups, or roles. Write them around the problem.

▷ **Identify individuals associated to the institutions**: Put the names of 2-3 individuals to the identified institutions. Put these names in the next circle around the problem.

▷ **Map other associates with the individuals**: Sometimes you have no direct access or connection to the identified individuals. Therefore, identify people who are related to them. Also note down, how they relate to the individual. Example: Colleagues, mentor, family member, neighbors, etc. Add and connect them to the network in the third ring.

▷ **Determine relational power lines**: Identify who relates to whom, and how they are influencing each other. Draw lines and add the direction of influence.

▷ **Target priority relationship**: Identify the persons who have the most relational power lines directed to the target. These people are your priority. If you have no direct access to them, then you can try to find people who can influence this person.

▷ **Plan**: Based on the network you derive actions. Example: Talk to influencer x or ask influencer y to schedule a meeting with influencer z.

Figure 13.1 includes a schematic example of a power map. The map is clustered in circles. From inside to outside it contains, the topic (target), the institutions and roles who have the power to decide, the concrete decision makers, and the people you know who can influence the decision makers. Arrows indicate a (social) connection and the arrow direction indicates the direction of influence. Bold arrows indicate a strong influence. Unlike the schematic example, you should give the people concrete names.

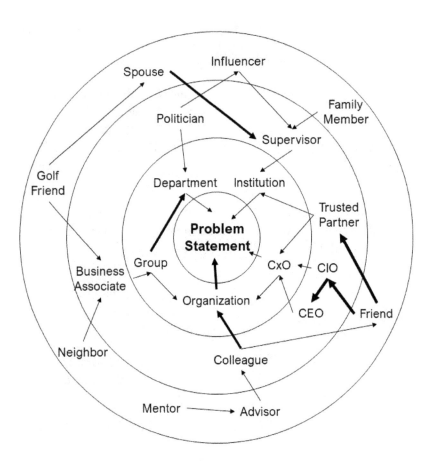

Figure 13.1.: Schematic example of a power map

Warning: Although all this can be used to make positive changes, there is always the risk to provoke or upset people. Be careful and avoid playing games with your promoters or detractors.

Benefit

The more complex your concepts are, the more difficult they are to implement. If you are an application architect, your team need to be convinced to support a specific concept or idea. If you are an enterprise architect, several more people and departments need to be convinced by a wider concept or idea. The wider the ideas are, the more support is required. Thus, it is not only beneficial to have allies, but they are sometimes even a prerequisite.

Also identifying detractors is important. Who does not like your idea, and why? What is necessary to convince them? Who is influencing those people, and how can you address their concerns?

With the power mapping tool, you can analyze and visualize the network which leads to decisions. The network can be used to influence the right people, to influence the decision makers, who then may decide or work in your favor. The benefit is obvious, you increase the chance to get what you want. But ask yourself, if you really want to take this path.

Example – Architecture CoP

In Section 12.3 the concept of CoPs was described. CoPs are an ideal way to find allies within an organization. If you regularly align with them, you can build a critical mass to influence and convince other people within the organization to adopt your practices and ideas.

Allies are beneficial, if you have a problem which you cannot solve by yourself. If you identify problems across the organization within a CoP, the chances are higher, that you can address these systemic issues to upper management and present solution options. The likelihood to fix a systematic, organization-overarching problem alone is small, but if many people from different departments or teams come together, the chances are high to change something.

The power mapping framework can also be used within a CoP. The more people you have, the more people you can address in the network to influence. For example, someone may have direct access to the CIO or some vendor contact. This may ease the work.

13.3. Repeat It, Believe It

Can you remember some marketing slogans from your youth regarding consumer goods, like sweets or toys? I guess that you can recall plenty. Maybe it was because of the fancy rhythms and rhymes of the slogans, or maybe because it was repeated over and over in TV, radio or billboards. And maybe you have observed yourself, while standing in the store and comparing products, that you preferred one product over the other because you have a better feeling about it. You assume it has better quality or that it offers more value.

If you repeat specific messages, people tend to believe them at some point in time. This may be only a subconscious influence, but it is an influence. And it can be very strong. When it comes to decisions, then the "gut feeling" will probably tend to the one, which feels more familiar.

So, if you really want to influence people, then this strategy is for you: You repeat your messages to all kind of people. Over and over. Whenever you see them. But they should not get bored from the same message: Wrap the message into different stories and have some variations.

Warning: This strategy is strong and can make a huge difference. But it is also dangerous. You are manipulating people's minds. And if people realize the evil within this strategy, they may hate you, ignore you or even throw you out. Thus, don't overdo it.

Important: Despite the warning: Talking about your ideas and opinions is important. You need to transport your messages to the right people. And a little bit of influencing is not evil, it's natural.

Benefit

You may ask, is this really working? Yes, there are many studies which confirm it. Just to mention one: "[...] studies show that repeated exposure to an opinion makes people believe the opinion is more prevalent, even if the source of that opinion is only a single person." [13] If you publish few messages often enough, it can help to convince people more easily.

Example – TINA Principle

You have a problem and a solution. No one really likes the solution as it has some nasty side effects. Everyone is making a fuss about your proposal, is blocking or even discrediting you. But your job is to solve and continue with work and you do not want to discuss anymore. Thus, you need to convince people, that this is the only solution which is feasible. There is no alternative to the solution. In short: You apply the TINA ("there is no alternative") principle [123].

Whenever you discuss about this specific or a similar topic, you mention, that your solution has no alternative. And it has been discussed in the past, over and over, always with the same result. The discussion is finished. And if they do not continue, a disaster will happen. Make it more colorful and underline the monstrous money the company will lose, and this will directly affect the bonus of everyone. Or that the project needs to be stopped and heads will roll. Or claim that experts in the field would do or are doing the same.

This strategy can suppress further discussions. Eventually, and this may take some time, people will believe, that there is no feasible alternative. Even if they have a good or even great alternative in mind, they will doubt the feasibility after some time. Too many people have already changed their mind. And they can hardly resist to also change it.

Margaret Thatcher, a former British prime minister, often used this phrase to stop debates about the downs of her political directions [11]. It was also used by the German chancellor Angela Merkel. The German word for having no alternative was even voted as the ugliest word of the year ("alternativlos"). "The word suggests objectively inappropriately that there are no alternatives in the decision-making process from the outset and thus no need for discussion and argumentation. Claims of this kind have been made too often in 2010, threatening to increase the disenchantment with politics among the population."[91]

Recently, I also was part of a similar TINA campaign. Initially, I was confused why they did what they did. I had good counter arguments and a proper alternative. In every meeting, in every discussion, I presented my alternative and pointed out the risks of the proposed solution. In the beginning I had some supporters. But after some time, as more and more people where influenced, even I got doubts. I reflected about it and realized what happened. But it was too late. Winning this discussion with arguments was not possible anymore.

13.4. Fight for your ideas and be persistent

People sometime do not like your ideas, or they are just too lazy to follow them. If you are really convinced by your ideas, you should continuously go after them and "fight". This is sometimes necessary. Architecture decisions with long term goals are often not the easiest one's: Developers do not like them, as they are more complex to develop. Managers do not like them, as they are more expensive in the short term. This is your job to be persistent and to negotiate.

Benefit

It seems, that there is no benefit in being persistent. You have a lot of resistance everywhere. And it would be easier, to just relax and let them do whatever they want. But honestly, if you want to move something, and really want to make a difference, then you need to fight. If the idea is worth it, and people are finally convinced to implement it, then this is a great achievement not only for you, but for the whole company.

Example – Process automation tool

Imagine, your company has decided to use a specific tool for process automation. You and your team should start to automate the first processes with it. At first, all are excited to be the first movers within the company. But quickly you realize, that the tool is not a good fit. Developers complain about the stability and bugs. Operations about the high demand of resources and slow processing speed. Senior management about the high license costs. You have many escalations about the outcome and progress. Additionally, the vendor is not as responsive and supportive with product issues as you need. The list is long, and you know that something needs to be changed.

You and your team made a research and found a better tool. More mature and a better fit for purpose. As architect you could now fight to get the new tool and migrate the old processes to the new. This has some costs and risks of course. But in the long run, everyone will be happier: Developers can increase their development speed, production would be more stable, and, by the way, you save a significant amount of license costs. You propose this to senior management, but they are resistant. They do not want to change. You could now give up and let it run... or fight.

The responsible architect decided to fight. He teamed up with several people: Other architects, developers, people from business and operations, mid and senior management, etc. He constantly demonstrated the capabilities of the new, preferred tool. He calculated business cases and did a SWOT analysis. He even gave a demo on a Raspberry Pi, to demonstrate the low resource consumption and speed of processing. Finally, the influence and pressure to try the new tool was high enough, that the next process was automated with the new tool, declared as a proof of concept. It was a success. And this success was sold on every occasion. Comparisons with the old tool were made: Time to market, resource consumption, response times of support, voices of involved people, etc. Eventually, the old processes were migrated, and the old tool was decommissioned.

Part IV.

Appendix

14. About the author

Dr.-Ing. Kai Niklas has been working for more than 15 years in the IT sector in various roles and different industries. Currently he helps clients in the finance sector as principal consultant to innovate in the role of a software architect. Kai is specialized in modern software architecture and agile software development practices, application integration, DevOps, business process automation and SAP for insurance. He has a broad background in software engineering and architecture in different roles: Software engineer, software architect, application architect, solution architect, integration architect, system engineer and enterprise architect. He studied mathematics, computer science and did his doctoral degree in the field of service-oriented architectures.

Connect with me on LinkedIn
(http://bit.ly/3029Tl9)

Bibliography

[1] Activiti. Open Source Business Automation, 2019. `https://www.activiti.org` [Online; accessed 03-May-2019].

[2] Jose Aguinaga. How it feels to learn JavaScript in 2016, 2016. `https://hackernoon.com/how-it-feels-to-learn-javascript-in-2016-d3a717dd577f` [Online; accessed 03-May-2019].

[3] Patrik Bostrom Andreas Rehn, Tobias Palmborg. The Continuous Delivery Maturity Model, 2013. `https://www.infoq.com/articles/Continuous-Delivery-Maturity-Model` [Online; accessed 03-May-2019].

[4] Angular. Angular - Style Guide, 2019. `https://angular.io/guide/styleguide` [Online; accessed 03-May-2019].

[5] Zachman International Enterprise Architecture. Zachman International - Enterprise Architecture, 2019. `https://zachman.com` [Online; accessed 01-March-2019].

[6] Solomon E Asch. Opinions and social pressure. *Scientific American*, 193(5):31–35, 1955.

[7] Sigal G Barsade. The ripple effect: Emotional contagion and its influence on group behavior. *Administrative science quarterly*, 47(4):644–675, 2002.

[8] bbv software services. Clean Code Cheat Sheet, 2019. `https://www.bbv.ch/images/bbv/pdf/downloads/V2_Clean_Code_V3.pdf` [Online; accessed 19-February-2019].

[9] Kent Beck. *Test-driven development: by example*. Addison-Wesley Professional, 2003.

[10] Kent Beck and C. Andres. *Extreme Programming Explained: Embrace Change*. XP Series. Pearson Education, 2004.

[11] Claire Berlinski. *There is no alternative: Why Margaret Thatcher matters*. Hachette UK, 2011.

[12] Barry Boehm, Chris Abts, A Winsor Brown, Sunita Chulani, Bradford K Clark, Ellis Horowitz, Ray Madachy, Donald J Reifer, and Bert Steece. Cost estimation with cocomo ii. *ed: Upper Saddle River, NJ: Prentice-Hall*, 2000.

[13] The Financial Brand. Say It Again: Messages Are More Effective When Repeated, 2018. https://thefinancialbrand.com/42323/advertising-marketing-messages-effective-frequency/ [Online; accessed 16-July-2018].

[14] M. Bremer. *How to Do a Gemba Walk: Coaching Gemba Walkers*. Independently Published, 2018.

[15] Camunda. BPMN Examples: Best Practices for creating BPMN 2.0 process diagrams., 2019. https://camunda.com/bpmn/examples [Online; accessed 28-February-2019].

[16] Camunda. Workflow and Decision Automation Platform, 2019. https://camunda.com [Online; accessed 03-May-2019].

[17] Ann Cass, C Volcker, Philipp Sutter, Alec Dorling, and Hans Stienen. Spice in action-experiences in tailoring and extension. In *Proceedings. 28th Euromicro Conference*, pages 352–360. IEEE, 2002.

[18] Mike Cohn. *Agile estimating and planning*. Pearson Education, 2005.

[19] Bonner Curriculum. Power Mapping: A Tool for Utilizing Networks, 2019. https://www.results.org/wp-content/

`uploads/bonnner_powermapping.pdf` [Online; accessed 24-March-2019].

[20] Shai Danziger, Jonathan Levav, and Liora Avnaim-Pesso. Extraneous factors in judicial decisions. *Proceedings of the National Academy of Sciences*, 108(17):6889–6892, 2011.

[21] The Agile Dictionary. Spike, 2019. `http://agiledictionary.com/209/spike/` [Online; accessed 12-February-2019].

[22] Susanne Diekelmann and Jan Born. The memory function of sleep. *Nature Reviews Neuroscience*, 11(2):114, 2010. `https://www.ncbi.nlm.nih.gov/pubmed/20046194` [Online; accessed 15-February-2019].

[23] George T. Doran. There's a S.M.A.R.T. way to write management's goals and objectives. In *Management Review*, volume 70, pages 35–36, 1981. `https://community.mis.temple.edu/mis0855002fall2015/files/2015/10/S.M.A.R.T-Way-Management-Review.pdf` [Online; accessed 03-May-2019].

[24] Elastic. ELK Stack, 2019. `https://www.elastic.co/elk-stack` [Online; accessed 30-January-2019].

[25] Forbes. What Does VUCA Really Mean?, 2018. `https://www.forbes.com/sites/jeroenkraaijenbrink/2018/12/19/what-does-vuca-really-mean/` [Online; accessed 12-February-2019].

[26] Martin Fowler. StranglerApplication, 2004. `https://www.martinfowler.com/bliki/StranglerApplication.html` [Online; accessed 05-April-2019].

[27] Martin Fowler. ModelDrivenSoftwareDevelopment, 2008. `https://martinfowler.com/bliki/ModelDrivenSoftwareDevelopment.html` [Online; accessed 27-February-2019].

[28] Martin Fowler, Kent Beck, John Brant, William Opdyke, and Don Roberts. *Refactoring: improving the design of existing code*. Addison-Wesley Professional, 1999.

[29] Jonathan L Freedman and Scott C Fraser. Compliance without pressure: the foot-in-the-door technique. *Journal of personality and social psychology*, 4(2):195, 1966.

[30] Erich Gamma. *Design patterns: elements of reusable object-oriented software*. Pearson Education India, 1995.

[31] Michael W Godfrey and Daniel M German. On the evolution of lehman's laws. *Journal of Software: Evolution and Process*, 26(7):613–619, 2014.

[32] Jorge Gomes, Mario Romao, and Mario Caldeira. Linking benefits to maturity models. 04 2013.

[33] The Open Group. TOGAF | The Open Group, 2019. `https://www.opengroup.org/togaf` [Online; accessed 01-March-2019].

[34] Teresa Hagan and David Smail. Power-mapping-i. background and basic methodology. *Journal of Community & Applied Social Psychology*, 7(4):257–267, 1997.

[35] John Harrison. Use templates for better Git commit messages, 2019. `https://engineering.autotrader.co.uk/2018/06/11/use-templates-for-better-commit-messages.html` [Online; accessed 28-February-2019].

[36] Martin Haussmann. *UZMO-Denken mit dem Stift: Visuell präsentieren, dokumentieren und erkunden*. Redline Wirtschaft, 2014.

[37] Gregor Hohpe. *37 Things One Architect Knows About IT Transformation: A Chief Architect's Journey*. 2016.

[38] Gregor Hohpe. The Architect Elevator - Visiting the upper floors, 2017. `https://martinfowler.com/articles/`

`architect-elevator.html` [Online; accessed 04-March-2019].

[39] Gregor Hohpe and Bobby Woolf. *Enterprise integration patterns: Designing, building, and deploying messaging solutions.* Addison-Wesley Professional, 2004.

[40] IBM. Rational Unified Process, 2019. `http://files.defcon.no/RUP` [Online; accessed 03-May-2019].

[41] Scaled Agile Inc. Community of Practice, 2019. `https://www.scaledagileframework.com/communities-of-practice` [Online; accessed 26-March-2019].

[42] Informatica. ActiveVOS, 2019. `http://www.activevos.com` [Online; accessed 03-May-2019].

[43] Stephen H. Kan. *Metrics and Models in Software Quality Engineering.* Addison-Wesley, 2003.

[44] Sam Kaner. *Facilitator's guide to participatory decision-making.* John Wiley & Sons, 2014.

[45] Svyatoslav Kotusev. The critical scrutiny of TOGAF, 2016. `https://www.bcs.org/content/conWebDoc/55892?changeNav=10130` [Online; accessed 01-March-2019].

[46] Philippe Kruchten. *The Rational Unified Process: An Introduction.* The Addison-Wesley object technology series. Addison-Wesley, 2004.

[47] Adam Lashinsky. The Cook Doctrine at Apple, 2009. `http://fortune.com/2009/01/22/the-cook-doctrine-at-apple/` [Online; accessed 22-March-2019].

[48] Klaus Leopold. *Practical Kanban: From Team Focus to Creating Value.* 2017.

[49] Marko Leppänen, Simo Mäkinen, Samuel Lahtinen, Outi Sievi-Korte, Antti-Pekka Tuovinen, and Tomi Männistö. Refactoring-a shot in the dark? *IEEE Software*, 32(6):62–70, 2015. https://ieeexplore.ieee.org/abstract/document/7310989 [Online; accessed 17-February-2019].

[50] Elizabeth F Loftus and John C Palmer. Reconstruction of automobile destruction: An example of the interaction between language and memory. *Journal of verbal learning and verbal behavior*, 13(5):585–589, 1974.

[51] David H Maister, Charles H Green, and Robert M Galford. *The trusted advisor*. Simon and Schuster, 2000.

[52] Robert C Martin. *Clean code: a handbook of agile software craftsmanship*. Pearson Education, 2009.

[53] Robert C. Martin. The Cycles of TDD, 2014. https://blog.cleancoder.com/uncle-bob/2014/12/17/TheCyclesOfTDD.html [Online; accessed 16-April-2019].

[54] Robert C Martin. *Clean architecture: a craftsman's guide to software structure and design*. Prentice Hall Press, 2017.

[55] Abraham Harold Maslow and Arthur G Wirth. The psychology of science: A reconnaissance. 1966.

[56] T. J. McCabe. A complexity measure. *IEEE Transactions on Software Engineering*, SE-2(4):308–320, Dec 1976.

[57] Geoffrey Moore. Using Innovation to Thrive and Strive, 2010. https://www.slideshare.net/sasindia/keynote-geoffrey-mooreusinginnovationtothriveandstrive [Online; accessed 16-March-2019].

[58] Geoffrey Moore. Digital Transformation: A Stairway to Heaven, 2017. https://www.linkedin.com/pulse/digital-systems-maturity-model-geoffrey-moore [Online; accessed 23-March-2019].

[59] Geoffrey A Moore. *Crossing the Chasm: Marketing and Selling Disruptive Products to Mainstream Customers.* Harper Collins, 1999.

[60] Netflix. Chaos Monkey, 2019. `https://github.com/Netflix/chaosmonkey` [Online; accessed 16-April-2019].

[61] Kai Niklas. *Verbesserung des Entwurfs von SOA Serviceschnittstellen mit Hilfe von Erfahrungen und Heuristiken.* Logos Verlag Berlin GmbH, 2017.

[62] Kai Niklas. CI/CD with Angular 6 & Firebase & GitLab, 2018. `https://hackernoon.com/ci-cd-with-angular-6-firebase-gitlab-5118ad469e4d` [Online; accessed 16-April-2019].

[63] Kai Niklas. Big Design Up Front, 2019. `https://en.wikipedia.org/wiki/Big_Design_Up_Front` [Online; accessed 16-April-2019].

[64] Ralph-Christian Ohr. Centralizing vs. Decentralizing Innovation, 2019. `http://integrative-innovation.net/?p=2208` [Online; accessed 20-March-2019].

[65] Gerard O'Regan. *Introduction to Software Quality.* Undergraduate Topics in Computer Science. Springer International Publishing, 2014.

[66] Andrew J Oswald, Eugenio Proto, and Daniel Sgroi. Happiness and productivity. *Journal of Labor Economics*, 33(4):789–822, 2015.

[67] Bart Perkins. IT mission, vision and values statements: Foundations for success, 2018. `https://www.cio.com/article/2448399` [Online; accessed 22-March-2019].

[68] Ruben Picek and Vjeran Strahonja. Model driven development-future or failure of software development. Citeseer.

[69] Daniel H Pink. *Drive: The surprising truth about what motivates us.* Penguin, 2011.

[70] RAML. RAML, 2019. `https://raml.org` [Online; accessed 03-May-2019].

[71] Donald G Reinertsen. *The principles of product development flow: second generation lean product development,* volume 62. Celeritas Redondo Beach, 2009.

[72] Ralf H. Reussner and Wilhelm Hasselbring. *Software architect.* dpunkt.verlag, 2008. `http://www.handbuch-softwarearchitektur.de/` [Online; accessed 16-July-2018].

[73] M. Richards. *Microservices Antipatterns and Pitfalls.* O'Reilly Media, 2016.

[74] Casey Rosenthal, Lorin Hochstein, Aaron Blohowiak, Nora Jones, and Ali Basiri. *Chaos Engineering.* O'Reilly Media,, 2017.

[75] Inc. Scaled Agile. Wighted Shortest Job First, 2019. `https://www.scaledagileframework.com/wsjf/` [Online; accessed 05-April-2019].

[76] Kurt Schneider. *Experience and knowledge management in software engineering.* Springer Science & Business Media, 2009.

[77] Deep Shah. The Ivory Tower Architect, 2011. `http://www.gitshah.com/2011/01/ivory-tower-architect.html` [Online; accessed 16-April-2019].

[78] Signavio. BPMN Modeling Guidelines, 2019. `https://www.modeling-guidelines.org` [Online; accessed 28-February-2019].

[79] Smartbear. Swagger, 2019. `https://swagger.io` [Online; accessed 03-May-2019].

[80] Switzerland SonarSource S.A. Continuous Inspection | Sonar-Qube, 2019. https://www.sonarqube.org [Online; accessed 16-April-2019].

[81] TheWealthHike. The Comfort Zone, 2018. https://www.thewealthhike.com [Online; accessed 03-May-2019].

[82] Nick T Thomopoulos. *Essentials of Monte Carlo simulation: Statistical methods for building simulation models.* Springer Science & Business Media, 2012.

[83] ThoughtWorks. Technology Radar, 2019. https://www.thoughtworks.com/radar [Online; accessed 03-May-2019].

[84] Herman Vantrappen. When to Decentralize Decision Making, and When Not To, 2017. https://hbr.org/2017/12/when-to-decentralize-decision-making-and-when-not-to [Online; accessed 20-March-2019].

[85] R. P. S. P. Veerraju, A. Srinivasa Rao, and G. Murali. Refactoring and its benefits. *AIP Conference Proceedings*, 1298(1):645–650, 2010. https://aip.scitation.org/doi/abs/10.1063/1.3516393 [Online; accessed 17-February-2019].

[86] Friedemann Schulz Von Thun. *Miteinander reden 1: Störungen und Klärungen: Allgemeine Psychologie der Kommunikation*, volume 1. Rowohlt Verlag GmbH, 2013.

[87] Ullrich Wagner, Steffen Gais, Hilde Haider, Rolf Verleger, and Jan Born. Sleep inspires insight. *Nature*, 427(6972):352, 2004.

[88] Etienne Wenger. *Communities of practice: Learning, meaning, and identity.* Cambridge university press, 1999.

[89] Wikipedia. Software architect, 2018. https://en.wikipedia.org/wiki/Software_architect [Online; accessed 16-July-2018].

[90] Wikipedia. 5 Whys, 2019. https://en.wikipedia.org/wiki/5_Whys [Online; accessed 02-March-2019].

[91] Wikipedia. Alternativlos, 2019. `https://de.wikipedia.org/wiki/Alternativlos` [Online; accessed 28-March-2019].

[92] Wikipedia. Capability Maturity Model Integration, 2019. `https://en.wikipedia.org/wiki/Capability_Maturity_Model_Integration` [Online; accessed 03-May-2019].

[93] Wikipedia. CMMI Institute, 2019. `https://cmmiinstitute.com/` [Online; accessed 03-May-2019].

[94] Wikipedia. COCOMO, 2019. `https://en.wikipedia.org/wiki/COCOMO` [Online; accessed 06-March-2019].

[95] Wikipedia. Divide-and-conquer algorithm, 2019. `https://en.wikipedia.org/wiki/Divide-and-conquer_algorithm` [Online; accessed 16-February-2019].

[96] Wikipedia. Domain Driven Design, 2019. `https://en.wikipedia.org/wiki/Domain-driven_design` [Online; accessed 05-April-2019].

[97] Wikipedia. Enterprise architecture framework, 2019. `https://en.wikipedia.org/wiki/Enterprise_architecture_framework` [Online; accessed 01-March-2019].

[98] Wikipedia. Extreme Programming, 2019. `https://en.wikipedia.org/wiki/Extreme_programming` [Online; accessed 03-May-2019].

[99] Wikipedia. Four-sides model, 2019. `https://en.wikipedia.org/wiki/Four-sides_model` [Online; accessed 16-March-2019].

[100] Wikipedia. Function point, 2019. `https://en.wikipedia.org/wiki/Function_point` [Online; accessed 16-April-2019].

[101] Wikipedia. Group dynamics, 2019. `https://en.wikipedia.org/wiki/Group_dynamics` [Online; accessed 12-February-2019].

[102] Wikipedia. ISO/IEC 15504, 2019. `https://en.wikipedia.org/wiki/ISO/IEC_15504` [Online; accessed 03-May-2019].

[103] Wikipedia. ISO/IEC 9126, 2019. `https://en.wikipedia.org/wiki/ISO/IEC_9126` [Online; accessed 10-January-2019].

[104] Wikipedia. Law of large numbers, 2019. `https://en.wikipedia.org/wiki/Law_of_large_numbers` [Online; accessed 11-March-2019].

[105] Wikipedia. Lehman's laws of software evolution, 2019. `https://en.wikipedia.org/wiki/Lehman%27s_laws_of_software_evolution` [Online; accessed 16-April-2019].

[106] Wikipedia. Lehman's laws of software evolution, 2019. `https://en.wikipedia.org/wiki/Business_Process_Model_and_Notation` [Online; accessed 16-April-2019].

[107] Wikipedia. Map Reduce, 2019. `https://en.wikipedia.org/wiki/MapReduce` [Online; accessed 16-February-2019].

[108] Wikipedia. Model-driven engineering, 2019. `https://en.wikipedia.org/wiki/Model-driven_engineering` [Online; accessed 16-April-2019].

[109] Wikipedia. Model view controller, 2019. `https://en.wikipedia.org/wiki/Model-view-controller` [Online; accessed 03-May-2019].

[110] Wikipedia. Model view viewmodel, 2019. `https://en.wikipedia.org/wiki/Model-view-viewmodel` [Online; accessed 03-May-2019].

[111] Wikipedia. Monte Carlo method, 2019. `https://en.`

wikipedia.org/wiki/Monte_Carlo_method [Online; accessed 03-May-2019].

[112] Wikipedia. Müller-Lyer illusion, 2019. https://en.wikipedia.org/wiki/M%C3%BCller-Lyer_illusion [Online; accessed 16-April-2019].

[113] Wikipedia. Object-oriented analysis and design, 2019. https://en.wikipedia.org/wiki/Object-oriented_analysis_and_design [Online; accessed 05-April-2019].

[114] Wikipedia. Occam's razor, 2019. https://en.wikipedia.org/wiki/Occam%27s_razor [Online; accessed 03-May-2019].

[115] Wikipedia. Power mapping, 2019. https://en.wikipedia.org/wiki/Power_mapping [Online; accessed 24-March-2019].

[116] Wikipedia. Quicksort, 2019. https://en.wikipedia.org/wiki/Quicksort [Online; accessed 16-April-2019].

[117] Wikipedia. Rational Unified Process, 2019. https://en.wikipedia.org/wiki/Rational_Unified_Process [Online; accessed 03-May-2019].

[118] Wikipedia. Reactive programming, 2019. https://en.wikipedia.org/wiki/Reactive_programming [Online; accessed 12-February-2019].

[119] Wikipedia. SMART Criteria, 2019. https://en.wikipedia.org/wiki/SMART_criteria [Online; accessed 03-May-2019].

[120] Wikipedia. Software quality, 2019. https://en.wikipedia.org/wiki/Software_quality [Online; accessed 10-January-2019].

[121] Wikipedia. SWOT analysis, 2019. https://en.wikipedia.org/wiki/SWOT_analysis [Online; accessed 12-February-2019].

[122] Wikipedia. The Open Group Architecture Framework, 2019. `https://en.wikipedia.org/wiki/The_Open_Group_Architecture_Framework` [Online; accessed 01-March-2019].

[123] Wikipedia. There is no alternative, 2019. `https://en.wikipedia.org/wiki/There_is_no_alternative` [Online; accessed 28-March-2019].

[124] Wikipedia. Volatility, uncertainty, complexity and ambiguity, 2019. `https://en.wikipedia.org/wiki/Volatility,_uncertainty,_complexity_and_ambiguity` [Online; accessed 03-May-2019].

[125] Wikipedia. We choose to go to the Moon, 2019. `https://en.wikipedia.org/wiki/We_choose_to_go_to_the_Moon` [Online; accessed 03-May-2019].

[126] Wikipedia. Zachman Framework, 2019. `https://en.wikipedia.org/wiki/Zachman_Framework` [Online; accessed 01-March-2019].

[127] Stefan Wolpers. Scrum Anti-Patterns Guide, 2019. `https://age-of-product.com/scrum-anti-patterns` [Online; accessed 05-April-2019].

[128] WordPress. WordPress - About Us, 2019. `https://wordpress.com/about/` [Online; accessed 30-January-2019].

[129] Zalando. Zalando Tech Radar, 2019. `https://opensource.zalando.com/tech-radar` [Online; accessed 03-May-2019].

[130] Caroline F Zink, Yunxia Tong, Qiang Chen, Danielle S Bassett, Jason L Stein, and Andreas Meyer-Lindenberg. Know your place: neural processing of social hierarchy in humans. *Neuron*, 58(2):273–283, 2008. `https://www.ncbi.nlm.nih.gov/pmc/articles/PMC2430590/` [Online; accessed 12-February-2019].

Bibliography

176

www.ingramcontent.com/pod-product-compliance
Lightning Source LLC
Chambersburg PA
CBHW070948050326
40689CB00014B/3389